James Payn

A Woman's Vengeance

Vol. 3

James Payn

A Woman's Vengeance
Vol. 3

ISBN/EAN: 9783337346515

Printed in Europe, USA, Canada, Australia, Japan

Cover: Foto ©Thomas Meinert / pixelio.de

More available books at **www.hansebooks.com**

A WOMAN'S VENGEANCE.

A Novel.

BY THE AUTHOR OF

"CECIL'S TRYST," "LOST SIR MASSINGBERD,"

ETC., ETC.

IN THREE VOLUMES.

VOL. III.

LONDON:
RICHARD BENTLEY AND SON.
1872.

CONTENTS OF VOL. III.

Contents.

A WOMAN'S VENGEANCE.

CHAPTER I.

IN HOSPITAL.

HITE beds, bare walls, carpetless floors, strange noiseless figures bending over beds — " Hush, hush!" What did all this mean? thought Arthur Tyndall, coming to himself after days that seemed weeks in the ward at Brignon Hospital; and where was he, and what had happened? Some accident, for he felt stiff and bruised all over, and could scarce stir a limb, and there were bandages about him. It was an effort even to keep his eyes open, and he closed them again ; besides, it was easier to think when they were shut.   Wherever he was, he had not been left alone ; far from it.   Streams of people had been to see him—rivers, seas, wave after wave of them.   Allardyce, for one, which was curious, considering what had happened between them ; and Paul Jones, with an ace of spades up his sleeve, which he pulled up and down to show it him for his amusement.   Uncle Magus, too, had brought his pistols with him for the same purpose, and had described to him how he had shot the Frenchman with one of them, which was imprudent of the old gen-tleman, considering that they *were* in France—in France, yes—but whereabouts ? Well, perhaps that would come presently. Let us think, think, think.   There's a bell tolling, which means that somebody's dead. *Well, perhaps you had better drive yourself, then !* Who said *that ?* Once more he opened his eyes—this time in alarm, for the voice had been very loud—and whom should they light upon, sitting beside him, with a very grave face, but Jack Adair!

"Dear Jack," said Arthur; "so good of you;" and then, as though it were the most natural thing in the world, he began to cry. He was neither ashamed nor astonished at himself; but what did astonish him, even at that weak and wretched pass to which he had been reduced, was that Jack cried too—Jack, whom he had never seen moved to tears; Jack, who, although of tender heart, was the last man in the world to "give way," or exhibit sentiment in a sentimental shape—Jack cried like a child. Why should Jack cry? It touched him, no doubt, to find his friend in hospital, and in such evil case, and to hear what had befallen him. But there again was the hitch. What *had* befallen him? What had he been doing? Where had he been going? *Well, perhaps you had better drive yourself, then!*

"You have said that twice, old fellow," said Jack softly.

Had he? Now, that was curious, for those were the very words that he himself had used to Helen before the carriage was upset.

That ray of consciousness was too much for him; it seemed as though a too great light had been let into his brain, and dazed it. He sank again into stupor, thence to sleep, and when he woke, the day had far advanced. But Jack was watching beside him as before—dear, faithful Jack, who had come (doubtless) post-haste from England for that very purpose. But there were no tears now; Arthur felt much stronger, and his mind was clearer far.

" How is Helen ?"

Perhaps Jack did not hear; at all events, he did not answer.

" Where is my wife ?"

" Here; under this roof," was the grave reply.

" Was she badly hurt ?"

" Yes."

" Poor soul ! poor soul ! Tell me about it," said Arthur.

" Nay, *we* know nothing, except that you were both brought here, much hurt. You were pitched out on your head, and had concussion of the brain."

" And Helen ?"

" The same."

How very short Jack's answers were. But then, as he had said, he had nothing to tell.

" It happened in this way," said Arthur. " We were coming very fast down the hill, and Helen said : ' Take care.' That was the first word she had spoken throughout the drive ; but then, it is true, I had not spoken either. We were not on good terms, Jack, nor had we been for months."

" Hush, hush ! For Heaven's sake, do not talk of that now."

" Very good ; I won't. I am very sorry it was so. I will make an effort—now that this has happened—to change all that. I will do my very best. Helen shall see——"

" How did it happen, Arthur ?" interrupted Adair, nervously. "Keep to that, if you can, and if trying to think it out does not hurt you. What took place after she said 'Take care'?"

"Well, that annoyed me. I knew how to drive well enough, of course; and it is disagreeable to be interfered with. And then to think that that should be the *first* time she had opened her lips to me. So, *'Perhaps you had better drive yourself,'* said I ; and I made as though I would have handed over the reins to her."

"Great Heavens!" ejaculated Adair, with horror. "And did she take them ?"

"No ; but it made me inattentive to the horses—reckless ; and just then something happened to frighten them on the roadside, and they ran up the bank, and, as I suppose, spilt us."

"That will do for to-night, Arthur; you look a little feverish. I will come again to-morrow morning."

"Thanks, old fellow. Pray, give my love to Helen. You have seen her to-day, have you not? They do let you see her, I hope; or is she too ill?"

" I have not seen her," answered Jack, speaking with difficulty; his tongue seemed glued to his mouth. " She was placed in the female accident ward, you see; but Blanche saw her."

" Blanche here! Why, how is that? You two have not made a runaway match of it, have you?"

" No, no." Never was seen such a sickly smile upon Jack's face before. It was more mournful by far than his tears had been. " Blanche and her mother are both here. They left London the same day they got the news of your accident."

" To nurse Helen? How good of them, and of you too, Jack! Blanche may come here, I know; I have seen ladies here, visiting their friends. Bring her to-morrow; I do so long to hear about poor Helen."

Let us return to the Hotel with Adair.

Mrs. Ralph and Blanche occupy with him the same sitting-room that Arthur and Helen used, and for which, alas, they have now no occasion. They are both looking pale and wretched ; and even on the elder lady's face—who is scarcely more given to exhibit emotion in public than Jack himself —are traces of recent tears. They both look up from their needlework as he comes in ; but not even Blanche has a smile for him.

"*How* is he ?" they inquire, simultaneously, with anxiety, but with much more of sadness, as one who, having been already struck by evil fortune, is somewhat numb to the second blow.

" Better ; he has come to himself, and told me how it all happened, and so forth."

"And did you tell *him?*" asked Blanche.

" I *could* not," replied Arthur, apologetically : " I dared not. I know it was very cowardly of me. I said *you* would come to-morrow.—I know what you are thinking, dear Mrs. Tyndall ; how it is always you poor women who are expected to say and do the unpleasant things. But Arthur is my oldest friend ; and Blanche knows so well how to approach—how to break such tidings. I might blurt it out and kill him."

" I will do my best," said Blanche, sobbing a little ; " but I think, dear mamma, that you would do it better."

" Well, I have prepared him to see you, Blanche," said Adair, "and I think, if your mother went, he would guess only too well what has happened.—What do *you* think, Mrs. Tyndall ? "

" I think Blanche had better go ; he is more used to her. But I shall accompany her to the hospital, of course. You and I, Mr. Adair, can stay below in the waiting-room."

"Shall I wear this, mamma ?" said Blanche, pointing to the work she was engaged on—some article of black crape. " The woman said our dresses would be home to-night."

" I think not, dear ; it might strike him

at once, then, and—— O poor Arthur!"
At this the tears of both women flowed
afresh, and Adair went to the window and
looked out for some minutes in silence : it
was a fine clear evening, but all seemed
mist to him.

The next day, Blanche went to see
Arthur, as had been arranged. But she
had over-estimated her self-control, and at
Arthur's first question, " How is Helen ?"
she remained speechless.

" Have you not seen her to-day,
Blanche ? "

She shook her head ; she tried to frame
some plausible excuse ; but the vision of
what she *had* seen but yesterday—the gaunt,
stiff form under the hospital sheet, that was
all that was now left of the blooming bride
of not a year ago—came into her mind,
and froze her speech.

" She is dead !" groaned Arthur, and
turned his face to the white wall.

It was no place for the luxury of grief;
the already crowded ward had received an

accession of new inmates, in consequence of
an accident occasioned by the collapse of
a circus tent in the town ; nor was Arthur's
sorrow of the sort to be assuaged by giving
vent to it. Not only regret, but something
very like remorse, was consuming him. The
last words he had uttered to his dead wife
had been peevish, if not passionate ; the
last look he had given her had been one of
displeasure, if not dislike. What would he
not have given to have recalled even those
last few minutes which they had spent together, and to have substituted another
look and other words for those he had
used ! He did not think of *her* share in
their estrangement, but only of his own.
He pictured her to himself at her very best
—happy, radiant, and devoted—as on the
day he married her.

"Did she suffer ?" asked he, presently,
in a voice so different from his own that it
might have emanated from some neighbour
patient—a ghostly voice that seemed to
be made up of echoes from the past.

"I trust not, Arthur; I think not. As I learn from the authorities here, she got better after the first day; they had great hopes indeed; and Maria was permitted to come and sit with her more than once. But on the night before we arrived, a sudden change for the worse took place— But I am torturing you."

"No, *no*," pleaded Arthur. "Tell me all. What I imagine for myself is far worse than aught you can have to say."

"There is little more to tell, Arthur. Maria saw her dear mistress *on* that night."

"She was quite herself in mind?"

"I—I think not, Arthur. She spoke very little about anything; but she seemed stronger, and had no fears about herself. Yet when Maria came here, as usual, the next morning, they told her that her mistress had passed away; and she went up-stairs and found it so. Judge of our horror, Arthur, to find such news as this awaiting us! The certificate of our dear one's death was sent that very day. I do believe

that all was done that could be done. But
only think of it—to have happened among
strangers in a room like this——" Her
sobs choked poor Blanche, and she hid her
face on Arthur's pillow.

"But you went yourself, Blanche, and
saw her?"

"O yes, as much as I dared to see,"
answered she, with a shudder. "Mamma
and I went to the little bed with her name
written upon the head of it—' Helen Tyndall'—which, I suppose, Maria had supplied, and we knelt down by it and bade
her good-bye."

"And *I* must see her and bid her good-
bye too, Blanche."

"That is impossible, Arthur; the doctor
told us it would kill you to be moved."

"Would to Heaven it would!" groaned
he. "That is all that is left for me now to
do—to die!"

Such an extremity of wretchedness was
in his face and tone, that Blanche was filled
not only with pity for him, but with a cer-

tain awe; the spectacle was more than she could bear alone.

"Mamma and Mr. Adair are below, Arthur; might I tell them to come up?"

He was still so weak and crippled that he could make no sign of acquiescence, and speech had once more failed him; but his eyes said "Yes." So Mrs. Ralph Tyndall and Adair were sent for. Upon the former he cast a grateful look, which she well understood; but it was no time for thanks.

"They tell me I cannot even see her," murmured he.

"No, dear Arthur, that is impossible; they say it will be days before you can leave your bed with safety. In the meantime, you know, you have only to express your wishes to myself or Mr. Adair, and everything shall be done in accordance with them."

"I am trying to think what *she* would have wished," he whispered. "Where is her poor mother?"

"We expect her every hour. I wrote to her at her London address directly I got

Maria's letter; but it seems she was out of town on a series of visits. They could not tell me for certain where she was, or when she would learn the news. Next to yourself, Arthur, my heart bleeds for *her*."

"*She* deserves your pity," replied Arthur, in a hollow voice; then, after a pause—"It is only right that her mother should decide; but I think she should be taken back to Swansdale."

"That seems fittest, Arthur; to her own home."

"Yes; but it was not a happy home," groaned the sick man. "Blanche—Jack—where are you?"

They came forward, standing each upon one side of the little bed.

Mrs. Ralph made a half-movement of disapproval; she apprehended what was coming, perhaps, but did not feel so certain of it as to justify her interference; or, perhaps, the circumstances of the case forbade it. At all events, there was no interruption to what followed.

" Blanche," said Arthur, with a tenderness as grave as that which haunts the tones of a dying man, " when *you* are married, you will have no cause to mistrust your husband ; but if a shadow of suspicion of his fidelity should ever threaten your bright days, put it from you, I beseech you, for it will darken the brightest. Jack—dear Jack, it would be out of place, indeed, should *I* give advice to *you ;* but I pray Heaven when you and Blanche are one— for that will be—that you may never have to reproach yourself on her account too late ; that *you* may never wish to recall look, speech, or thought of her—and wish in vain."

It was not until three days afterwards that Mrs. Somers arrived at Brignon, too late to see the last of her dead Helen. Even then, Arthur was not in a condition to be moved. So Adair remained to look after him ; while the two ladies, escorted by Mr. Glyddon, who came over for that purpose, journeyed to Swansdale with their sad charge. Blanche never forgot those three days' travel. Extreme wretchedness had induced in poor Mrs. Somers a sort of stupor, which necessitated Mrs. Ralph's whole attention and tendance, but none of the woful incidents of the way were spared to her daughter. The bereaved mother would not be separated from the coffin that held her dear one's remains, so the dead and the living journeyed by the same train. The shocks to which the feelings of Blanche were thus necessarily subjected at every break of line, and in the change from rail to steamboat, were very severe ; while the vulgar curiosity that their awful burden excited was to the last degree distressing. She had never been deeply attached to Helen, but she had been intimate with her, as girls of the same age about to be closely connected with one another naturally become, and her nerves were terribly jarred from first to last. The burial itself was far more trying than such sad scenes usually are, from the absence of him who should have been the chief-mourner, and its cause, as well as from the comparison that would intrude itself between the present and the time they had spent at Swansdale, such a little while ago, when she whom they now laid in her grave was a blooming girl in the happy anticipation of her bridal hour.

As Mrs. Somers insisted upon attending the funeral in person, Mrs. Ralph and Blanche could not do otherwise than bear her company; and when all was over, they carried the poor forlorn woman with them to their own home. Mrs. Ralph urged Uncle Magus to come also, but the old man pressed her hand, and shook his head, and in a faltering voice replied—" I shall not leave home, my dear, till I am carried yonder, whither *she* has gone so sadly soon." It seemed as though ten years of sorrow had fallen upon his gray head at once.

CHAPTER II.

AT THE MASQUERADE.

ADAIR'S attachment to Arthur Tyndall had needed no incentive, but the words that his friend had spoken upon his sick-bed to him and to Blanche had given him good cause for gratitude. Since Mrs. Ralph Tyndall had not gainsaid them at the time, nor alluded to them afterwards, he had reason for supposing that his attentions to her daughter would be no longer objected to. And indeed, so strong a term could scarcely at any time have been applied to that excellent lady's opposition to the young

2—2

people's wishes. It was Jack's own mo-
desty that had been the chief obstacle in
the matter. He was really getting on in
that profession of which the degrees of
comparison are said to be, " Hard to get
on, harder to get honour, hardest to get
honest;" and had he taken courage to set
forth his position and prospects to his dear
one's mamma, they would probably have
by no means appeared contemptible to her
sagacious vision : she had thought him
poorer than he was, though she had always
given him credit for those riches of the
heart which she so well knew how to value.
But it was his nature to attribute his success
to anything rather than his own merits,
and especially to the good offices of his
friend; and therefore, upon the receipt of
a certain spontaneous and most satisfactory
epistle from Mrs. Tyndall herself, upon a
subject that we can guess at, and which
also contained an allusion to Arthur's
words, he at once set down at least half his
good fortune as a debt he owed to Arthur.

If the latter had permitted him to discharge
it in so extravagant a fashion, he would
have sacrificed what was to him (for it was
the height of term-time) most valuable
time, in attendance upon his friend during
convalescence ; but the latter would not
hear of that, and so soon as he was able to
leave Brignon, a spot become hateful to
him from association, and remove to Brussels, whither he had been ordered by the
doctors, he dismissed Adair to Law and
Love.

Jack prospered in both ; and after some
months, conveyed to Arthur the news of
his approaching marriage, with the expression of an earnest hope that his friend
would find himself sufficiently recovered in
health and spirits to be present at it. He
received a letter in reply which shocked
him. There was no word in it of complaint or repining, and yet it was easy to
read in it that the writer was supremely
wretched. There was in particular an
attempt at cheerfulness in it, that to Adair,

who knew his friend so well, seemed to be
the language of a breaking heart.   Now
and then, though rarely, the bitterness that
lay beneath the jest shewed its sharp lines.
" You will not suppose, dear Jack, that I
cannot come because I am more pleasantly
engaged ; or that I will have nought to do
with marriage, or giving in marriage, because I am in heaven.   It is not quite
heaven, this living abroad—alone—among
strange scenes, which have nevertheless no
interest for me, and among strange people
who seem phantoms, so little has my flesh
and blood in common with them ; and yet
I feel it better to be here than at home.
There is at least nothing to remind me of
the Past—or *almost nothing.*   (When we
next meet—if we do meet—I will explain
these last two words, for they contain an
enigma.) . . . .   Next to the news of your
own happiness, the tidings of dear Mrs.
Somers' slow but sure recovery of her
usual health and spirits delight me.   How
I envy her these ' low beginnings of con-

tent.' . . . You speak of there being some
possibility of your making your marriage-
tour in this direction, in case I should still
be at Brussels. That is only like your old
kindness, and Blanche's. Of course I cannot say 'Don't come :' it will be bliss to
see you ; but, to tell you the honest truth,
I am not quite the company for a bride and
bridegroom. At all events, give me due
notice of your coming, that I may put a
wreath on my death's head."

Nothing more was heard of Arthur before the wedding, except that a very mag-
nificent present arrived for Blanche, from
Brussels.

"Why, it is fit for a queen !" exclaimed
she in expostulation at its splendour, but
with a beaming look, nevertheless ; for
what woman's eyes ever gazed on her own
diamonds without reflecting some portion
of their effulgence !

"That is why the dear old fellow has
sent them, because he knows you are my
queen," said Jack tenderly.

" At all events," said Blanche, " he must
have paid a royal price for them.—Must he
not, Mrs. Somers ?"

The old lady happened to be calling in
Eaton Square, where she was a frequent
and welcome visitor, when the tiara arrived.
Blanche's remark drew a most unexpected
reply from her.

" Yes, indeed, my dear, he must," assented she.   " And wherever the poor man
found the money—— But, O dear ! O
dear ! I forgot.   I've been and let it out,
and I promised not."   She wrung her
hands, and began to cry quite piteously.

" Pray, don't tell us anything, my dear
Mrs. Somers, that ought to be secret," observed Mrs. Tyndall, " or which it dis-
tresses you to reveal."   This good lady
was burning with curiosity, and therefore
deserved the greater credit for her scrupu-
lous delicacy.

" Oh, it don't distress me to *talk* about
it," said Mrs. Somers, " though it pained
me very much to have to do it : and since

I have once let it out of the bag, I can't put it back again, so you may just as well have it. We are all friends here, as the saying is, and I know it won't go no farther."

Her little audience looked adhesion to this sentiment, but none of them had any suspicion of the nature of the confidence that was about to he reposed in them.

" The fact is *this*, my dears," said Mrs. Somers (she had taken to call Jack "my dear" ever since his engagement), " Arthur Tyndall has done a very foolish thing. He was always generous in his way, poor fellow, whatever his short-comings, and when he married, it was more through my lawyer's doing than his own that he had even a life-interest secured to him on my dear Helen's property. He wanted it to be all tied up to her and hers. I think it very likely indeed (for he looked but little into business matters) that he concluded it was so ; but, at all events, when my poor darling died, he formally gave up what was his own, and insisted on my taking back at once whatever he had received with her on his marriage. Heaven knows, now she has gone, that *I* have no use for it, and so I told him; but he was as stiff as brocade about it, and not to be moved from his intention. It was very wrong of me to tell about it, since he particularly enjoined upon me not to do so; but when I saw that beautiful present, I couldn't help saying to myself, 'Why, where on earth did he get the money to buy it?' only—like a fool—I said it aloud."

At these words of Mrs. Somers, her three hearers were not only astonished, but distressed; Blanche on account of the magnificence of the present that had been made to her, and which it was now made plain the giver could ill afford; but her mother and lover for another reason, which pained them even more, though both forbore to mention it. They felt it was not pride, as good, easy Mrs. Somers imagined, which had prevented Arthur's reaping any advan-

tage from Helen's death, but the consciousness—overstrained and exaggerated though
it might be—of his own deficiencies as her
husband, and of the estrangement that had
taken place between them; and, coupling
this intelligence with his late letter, and
with what they had seen in him at Brignon,
they felt only too certain that his present
unhappiness was due to this morbid reflection, rather than to the mere sense of loss.
This conviction made Adair secretly more
resolved than ever to see, and, if possible,
comfort his old friend, upon the first opportunity, and accordingly Brussels was decisively fixed on as one of the places to be
visited on their marriage tour. The wedding took place, and, a few weeks afterwards, Mr. and Mrs. John Adair found
themselves in that town accordingly. In
consequence of an alteration in the trains,
they arrived at the *Hôtel du Parc*—where
they had ordered rooms, and where Arthur
himself was located—some hours before
they were expected, and he did not happen

to be within.   The place being new to
them, they went out for a stroll in the
Park, and presently sat down on one of
the seats of its broad walks.   There were
a good many promenaders, but one in particular attracted Adair's attention.   He was
a man of middle height, very thin, and, to
judge by his gray beard, considerably advanced in age, yet he walked at a pace so
quick that it could scarcely have been used
save by a young man.   Threading in and
out among the throng, he almost reminded
one of a skater, so rapid were his movements ; and yet, as it seemed, he had no
object in view but to reach the end of the
gravel-walk, and then come back again.

" That is some Englishman taking a constitutional," observed Jack, pointing him
out to Blanche.   " No wonder, judging
from such specimens, that foreigners think
us mad."

"Englishman, my dear husband!" gasped
Blanche—" that is Arthur himself."

" Heaven forbid ; it is impossible—and
yet——"

" Come away, John, pray," cried Blanche, excitedly; " if he were to come nearer, he would recognise *us* easily enough; you remember what he wrote about giving him notice of our arrival; I am sure he would rather meet us in the hotel."

Jack obeyed his bride, as in duty bound; but he could not help turning back on his way again and again to watch the spectral figure, which, changed as it was, he now recognised indeed for his old friend. That misery should have made him gray, even in so short a time, was barely possible, but what had given him that wild and wandering look?

" What *can* be the matter with him, Blanche ?"

" Sorrow and solitude, dear John, I fear," said she. "If *I* lost *you*, should not I look wan and wild ?"

Jack pressed his darling's arm in acknowledgment of her pretty speech, but, in truth, he could see little parallel in the two cases. It was no use, however, to speculate upon

the causes that had thus affected Arthur;
what he had to think of was the best means
to mitigate or remove them.   In this he
was more than seconded by Blanche herself.

"Remember, dearest Jack," said she,
"that though I can never be so happy as
with you alone, that there is nothing I
would not do for Arthur; and if you think
we can do him good by staying here, or by
taking him with us elsewhere, his company
will be always welcome to me."

As they were just then in that particularly open space called "the Plain," in front
of the *Hôtel du Parc*, Jack could not express his feelings in the way that would
have been most gratifying to both parties,
but he squeezed her soft plump arm again,
informed her (though not for the first time)
that she was an angel, and accepted with
gratitude the offer of her help.

"You have proposed the very plan that
has occurred to myself, Blanche, but which,
without your connivance, would have been

useless. It is from you, far more than from me, that Arthur's cure must come, if it comes at all. It is not in man to condole with his fellow on the loss of a wife, as woman can. Only, in this case, you must be very cautious. Poor Helen and Arthur did not pull quite so well together as man and wife as you and I shall do, darling (or if not, it will be my fault, not yours). And you remember what the dear fellow said to us at Brignon ?"

"Yes, yes," said Blanche; "I think I understand. Suppose I was to suggest, for instance, that, though an excellent husband in your way, you yourself have your eccentricities—are cold at times, and a little difficult to please; and that, in short, we are not without our quarrels. Then, if he shows surprise (as he well may), I will go on to hint that I am no worse off than other wives, nay, better (and that is surely true, John); that marriage is always more or less of a compromise——"

" I *must* kiss you, my darling, I really

must!" exclaimed Jack, in a transport. " I
knew I had married a sensible girl, but you
have the wits of all your sex combined!
You're a perfect Machiavelli; and all the
time as innocent as a ringdove! Yes, that's
exactly what you must make *him* feel—
that he made no worse a husband than
other men—and, upon my life, I don't believe he did; it was only that he and Helen
were singularly unsuited to one another.
If he had married Jenny——"

" Jenny? What! Arthur marry old
Jacob Renn's daughter?"

" No, no; I don't mean that—of course
not." ("She's a darling, and I still say,
has all the wits of her sex," muttered Jack
to himself, "but she has also one of their
weaknesses.") " I mean, if he had married
any girl who understood him, they would
have got on together capitally. While
speaking of poor Helen with all the praise
and kindness her memory deserves, try to
make him feel *that* also; that is the medicine, if I am not mistaken, for his morbid

thoughts. And now—for he will be here in a few minutes— not a word of our having seen him in the Park; and do not seem shocked or astonished at his changed appearance; and, please Heaven, we shall bring him right yet."

It was difficult, notwithstanding that they *had* seen him already, to express no surprise when they met Arthur; his haggard air, his nervous manner, his joyless tones, were so marked and conspicuous, directly the first emotion of pleasure, which this meeting with his old friends evoked, had subsided; but Blanche played her part to perfection, and, after a time, Arthur grew more at his ease; it was clear he had expected some remark to be expressed upon his changed appearance, and was relieved at its not having been made. He asked cordially after Mrs. Tyndall, and also after Uncle Magus, who was far from well (they did not tell him that the shock of Helen's death had been the chief cause of prostrating the old man); but his most anxious inquiries

were after Mrs. Somers. He seemed surprised, though well pleased, to hear that she
had regained so much of her old health and
spirits, and this offered an opportunity for
the two conspirators to speak a word in
season; how the loss of even those that
should be dearest to us can never be intended to cloud our whole lives long, and
if a Rachel weeping for her only child could
be thus comforted, and submit herself to
Fate's decree, so should a husband also.

These sentiments and reflections, of
course, were not intruded, nor fitted with
pointed personal application, but Arthur
evidently understood their drift. He did
not attempt to combat them, but listened
in silence, with a sort of affectionate sadness, that showed he was grateful for the
kindness that prompted them. Not until
Blanche had retired to her room, and Jack
produced the pipes and tobacco—for his
bride was far too wise a woman to deprive
her husband of that solace; her mission,
she justly thought, was to increase his joys,

and not diminish them—did Arthur let fall a word about his own condition. It was in answer to a question from Adair, " When are you coming back to us in England, old fellow ?" that he looked up into his friend's face, and slowly said : "All places are alike to me, Jack, now."

" But not all people," rejoined the other : "the warmness of your welcome to us to-day would alone disprove *that.*"

" Of course I am glad to see you and Blanche, Jack. O yes. I feel to-day for the first time since—since Helen's death, that I am still united by a strand or two to the rest of my fellow-creatures ; I had thought they had all parted, and that I was quite alone —quite alone !"

" You are doing yourself great harm, Arthur, leading this solitary life : at your age, you have no right thus to throw yourself away. I thought, when I left you here six months ago, that you had begun to look life in the face, and were plucking up some spirit."

"So I had, so I did, Jack," answered Arthur, in desponding tones. "I was getting better, wasn't I?"

"Of course you were; and why did not the improvement continue? That your sense of loss should have been keen was only to have been expected by those who knew you; your best friends would not have wished it otherwise; but the dead should not haunt the living for ever."

"They *do* haunt them—they *do*, Jack," answered Arthur, in low grave tones. His white face seemed to grow paler, his form more gaunt and thin, and each particular hair in his gray beard to stand out from the flesh, as he added: "I am a haunted man."

Adair was more than shocked; his heart sank within him at the sudden thought: "This man is mad." But he did not move a muscle, nor suffer his voice to lose its ordinarily cheerful tone, as he replied: "Well, we are all more or less haunted men, Arthur; and the more we shut ourselves out from those who were intended to be our fellow-creatures, and live in our own thoughts, the more ghosts we see."

" You are speaking of mere fancies, Jack. When I was shipwrecked and half-starved, I had fancies; though I was broad awake, I saw scenes with the inward eye—ay, and people too—quite as vividly as that in which I really was; but I knew that it was fancy, nevertheless."

"And what is it you see now, old fellow ?"

" Nothing *now*, thank Heaven ; but what I have seen I may see again to-night, to-morrow; and the fear of it, the terror of it, Jack, has made me what you see. Listen. It was about four months after you left me, and one before you wrote me word of your approaching marriage—and as you say, I was getting stronger and more cheerful; so far from courting solitude, as I do now, I felt inclined to mix with society, and when I did so, found myself the better for it. I had no friends

here—scarcely an acquaintance, indeed—so
that such gatherings as I frequented were
necessarily public ones.   Many persons
would perhaps have thought it somewhat
soon, after such a loss as I had suffered, to
be going about to concerts and theatres ;
for I have always taken my own way (as
you know) in social matters without much
thought of Mrs. Grundy, and I did so then.
When a masked ball in honour of Prince
Henry's birthday was announced at the
theatre, I even attended that, not for the
dancing's sake, for I did not mean to
dance, but because some acquaintances I
had made at the hotel happened to be
going thither, and persuaded me to accompany them."

"One moment," observed Jack, interrupting him.   "I don't wish to anticipate
you, though I think I know what is coming.
But were you conscious, in going to this
ball, that you were doing anything wrong ?
—I mean anything that jarred ever so little
upon your sense of what was right and

fitting in connection with your recent loss ? "

"I was not. I had been dining temperately with my friends, and went with them, just as I should have done to an ordinary concert or promenade; not with much expectation of being amused, yet not quite indifferently. I sat in one of the stage-boxes, on a level with the maskers, and observing them; when suddenly my attention was rivetted upon one with a black domino—Jack, I am telling you the truth, and no lie—whose gaze seemed to pierce me through and through."

"It was a woman, of course," said Jack, dryly.

"It was a woman, but not of flesh and blood. I should have known those eyes among a thousand, even if they had not been bent on me (as they were), with such a fierce yet reproachful look, as makes me shudder when I think of it. Jack, those were Helen's eyes !"

"You think so," said Adair, quietly.

" And yet, are you aware there is a game
played among children — called, I think,
Russian Buff—in which the faces of the
players are hidden, and only the eyes revealed, wherein the difficulty of recognition,
even with those best known to one another,
is found to be fully equal to that felt in the
English game of Blind Man, where the
eyes of the would-be recogniser are ban-
daged, and he has only the sense of touch
to help him ?"

" I know that, and yet I recognised those
eyes.   Nay, what is more, and worse, she
moved her mask aside for an instant, and
showed me Helen's face : pale, angry, cold,
as I had often seen it, and (Heaven help
me !) helped to make it.   Then, when I
sprang up in horror, though without a
word, for terror had paralysed my tongue,
she glided among the dancers, and disap-
peared."   Here he stopped, overcome by
deep emotion, and it was some moments
ere he could resume his narration.   " Ever
since that day I have lived in solitude, or

if, by chance, I mix with crowds, I move through them at speed, and gaze neither to left nor right, lest I should see that sight again. The remembrance of it is hateful to me ; the thought of it, ever present as it is, weighs on my spirits, and is eating away my life."

"So much is clear," said Jack, with gravity. "The effect, unhappily, can be seen by everybody ; but the cause, as I conclude—this spectral vision, if you will have it so—no other person saw except yourself."

"O yes ; two other men were in the box with me, and as I sprang up, followed the direction of my eyes, and saw it. To them, of course, it only seemed a woman masked."

"May I explain it ?" said Jack, smiling.

"Explain it! I would give all that I possessed, friend, if you or any other man could but do so," sighed Arthur, despairingly.

"Let me try, at all events," said Adair,

cheerfully. "You were not conscious of
any wrong-doing, you say, in going to this
masked ball; but, nevertheless, it was the
first scene of the kind which you had
visited since your great loss : there must,
therefore, have been some underlying sense
at least of incongruity in such a proceeding; the idea, 'How soon!' must have
crossed you, if only for an instant.   Did it
not ?"

"I have no recollection of it doing so,"
answered Arthur, with a faint smile of incredulity.

"Still, it may have done so ; and when
you suddenly found yourself gazing with
some interest at a pair of fine blue eyes,
your conscience smote you, though you
knew it not, by causing your thoughts to
instantly revert to Helen.   Your face at
the same time betrayed your thoughts;
and the young woman in the black domino,
taking it as a bad compliment, no doubt,
that you looked so weird and startled at
her, when she would have had you smile,

flashed rage and scorn at you.   Moreover,
to show you what a prize you had missed
by your ill-temper, she slipped her mask
aside, and let you see her face.   She would
be as much astonished, doubtless, as you
were yourself, to know she frightened you."

" But I *saw* her face, Jack : and though
it was but for an instant, the recognition
could not have been more complete had I
gazed at it for hours."

"It was not mutual, I suppose, however?"
said Jack, laughing.

" It *was*, so help me Heaven !" said
Arthur solemnly.   " If wonder, or caprice,
or any other easily aroused feeling, had
been the expression of the features, I
should have doubted, no matter how like
had been the face itself to that of Helen ;
but in place of those, there was a certain
awful significance which compelled belief—
a dread reproach and menace !   O Jack,"
cried the unhappy man with a shudder, and
putting his hand up as though to shut out
the vision he described, " I cannot bear to

speak of it! Your supposition, however cogent to yourself, must needs weigh light as air to me, who have seen with my own eyes. I beseech you let us talk of something else."

And the subject was dropped accordingly.

CHAPTER III.

AGAIN and again, on subsequent occasions, did Adair endeavour to lead the conversation towards this same topic, in hopes to shake the morbid conviction of his friend; but Arthur so obviously declined the argument as something not only distasteful but distressing, that he was obliged to abandon his good intent. Adair spent not only the rest of his honeymoon, but several weeks beyond it, at Brussels, and only left it when compelled by urgent business. It was plain that the presence of himself or Blanche

was not only grateful but beneficial to
Arthur, and they not only used their
utmost efforts to win him from his melancholy, but did their best to carry him off
with them to England. From Brussels,
however, he declined to move, and there
they left him, not without some grave misgivings not only for his health, but for his
reason. Blanche had indeed no hope of
ever seeing her cousin himself again ; and
though Jack thought he knew of a remedy
for his old friend, it could not be applied.
Months and months passed away, and only
by an occasional letter, uncomplaining as
usual, yet eloquent of gloom and wretchedness in its tone, did Arthur give sign of his
existence. Yet he was not forgotten by
faithful Jack ; and when talking of their
going out of town at Easter, " What do
you think, Blanche," said he, " of running
down to Swansdale for a week or two ? If
we proposed to do so, it is just possible
that Arthur might be induced to join us
there."

"Swansdale will be charming," replied Blanche delightedly—"that is, if we do but have bright weather—and though, in my opinion, his old home is the last place likely to prove attractive to one to whom the past is so painful, ask Arthur, by all means."

As Blanche had predicted, Arthur declined this invitation very positively; and though, in the same note in which he did so, he pressed him to use his house as their own home, the idea was not agreeable to them. Without its host, and with its recent unhappy associations, Swansdale Hall was not quite the place adapted for a holiday residence, so they took rooms at the *Welcome Inn.*

That spring chanced to set in as spring in England often does, with a foretaste of summer, afterwards to be compensated for, alas, by a relapse into winter. Tree and herb wore their brightest green; such flowers as there were gave forth their freshest fragrance; and the river danced in the sunlight, as though there were no bleak winds and leaden skies in store to ruffle and vex it. Jack and Blanche were on the water from bright morn to chilly eve ; they fished; they rowed, (and a very "pretty oar" Blanche looked, and *was*, let me tell you) ; they sketched. They took their honeymoon all over again, in short, and enjoyed it quite as much as the first one. Then suddenly, as though to remind them that they were mortals, to whom happiness without cloud is forbidden, a messenger from the Hall arrived with evil news. Uncle Magus, with whom they had dined but the day before (he had not been well enough throughout the winter to leave his own roof), had been taken suddenly very ill. On arriving at the cottage, they found these tidings only too well confirmed. He had had a paralytic stroke, which, although he was already recovering from its immediate effects, the doctor told them would be fatal. If he had not possessed a constitution of iron, grief for his son's fate would long ago have killed him ; it had survived that, and the

many years of solitude and bitter thoughts
which had followed it; it had survived, too,
his favourite Helen's death, but the shock
had weakened the old man, and left him
with little strength to bear any attack of
disease. Yet even now his will was as in-
domitable as ever. His chief solicitude
seemed to be as to whether the effects of
the paralysis would be confined to the left
side, where it had taken place; and would
therefore leave his right arm free to pursue
the task in which he had been of late engaged. The approach of death, of which
he was quite cognizant, filled him with no
alarms; his only apprehension was, that
there would be no time to finish that great
legacy to posterity—his manuscript on the
Duello. He would have sat up in bed, to
consult authorities, and jot down notes,
even now, and could only be restrained
from doing so by the argument that his
object would be defeated by the very means
he would have taken to effect it.

" He cannot live ten days in any case,"

was the doctor's verdict : whereupon Adair
drove round to the railway station on his
way back to the inn that night, and telegraphed for Arthur.

"If *that* be finished," Uncle Magus had
said, referring to his *magnum opus*, " and if
I could but see Arthur before I die, there
would be nothing else to wait for." The
last part of that speech was read in Brussels
next morning word for word ; and, as
Adair had expected, they brought Arthur
to Swansdale Hall within two days, or as
fast as steam could bring him. He took
up his quarters at the Hall, alone, though
Jack pressed his coming to the *Welcome*,
but tended his relative day and night as-
siduously.

" I did not know you at first," said the
old man with tender frankness, " but I know
you now ; there is no hand so kind, no voice
so dear to me as yours, Arty, nor ever has
been since I lost my own poor boy."

Arthur was indeed but the shadow of his
former self—perceptibly thinner and more

aged even than when last seen at Brussels; but his bodily health seemed good, and his plans for the future had, it seemed, at last taken some shape.

" I am going," said he to Adair, " whither I ought to have gone two years ago, and would to Heaven I had! So soon as Uncle Magus has bidden us farewell, I leave England for ever."

" But for what place ?"

" That is no matter, so long as it is somewhere, far removed from home and all its cruel associations—South America, perhaps. I shall take the first ship from Liverpool that promises the farthest voyage."

" You have had, I trust, no recurrence of that painful fancy ?" inquired Jack, softly, and after a long silence.

" I have not," said Arthur, " if, at least, (as I suppose), you mean by ' fancy' a sight as real and infinitely more terrible than this death-bed, to which you have summoned me. No, Jack, no; I have seen Helen's face no more."

4—2

"Nor ever will see it, dear friend," urged Jack, "unless in heaven."

But Arthur returned no answer; it was plain that his hallucination on that point was as confirmed as ever.

Though Uncle Magus had rallied for a day or two, he was now clearly dying; but still he would insist on being taken out of bed, and clothed so far as it was possible, in order that he might sit in his old arm-chair with his desk and manuscript before him. He spoke seldom, but always to the purpose, to the last. "Let my poor boy be buried with me," he had said, pointing to the embalmed body of his son, which had been the companion of his solitude for more than a quarter of a century; "and all I have to leave is yours, Arty"—"Arty" had been his pet name for Arthur as a boy, now unconsciously resumed after those many years; "the title-deeds, you know," he added, "are yours by right."

If he had ever really given up the idea that these were of great value, which is

doubtful, it revived in him now. All his
old associations did so, to judge by the
snatches of speech which he uttered when
his eyes were closed and he thought himself alone. Once he burst out with—" By
George, I've missed him!" in accents of in-
tense disappointment; and once he cried,
" Starved, starved, starved!" in a tone that
chilled his hearers' hearts.

A pagan, suckled in a creed outworn,
though he was, and one to whom the world
he was about to enter could scarcely be
more strange to him than that which he
was leaving, he had his sympathies and
affections. His views about " ancestry "
and " blood " indeed may have been as
worthless as those proclaimed by the merest
parvenu in a club, or any female tuft-hunter
who manœuvres for a lord at her Baker
Street dinner-table, but there was this difference—his were genuine; he believed in
them as he did in his own existence; and
what there ever had been of courage and
chivalry inherent in those accidents which

he deemed virtues, he possessed.   In bed
he refused to stay even to the very last,
and died, as it were, in harness, feebly
holding the feeble pen with which he would
have defended an old-world and died-out
custom.

   " Arrived at the Releager (or appointed
place)"—were the last words he wrote, ere
he himself was removed to *his* Releager.
The dying warrior that bade his sons put
on his armour, and set him on his war-
horse, that he might die as he had lived,
was a type of him ; but stern and ungenial
as he was, Uncle Magus left those behind
him who loved him and mourned his loss.
He was laid, with his long dead son beside
him, close to Helen's grave, in accordance
with his own express desire.

   It was the first occasion on which Arthur
Tyndall had appeared in public since his
return, and the appearance of the widower
was such that not a few of the spectators
shook their heads and remarked beneath
their breath, that it would not be long be-

fore the squire followed his young wife to Swansdale churchyard.

He was to remain but one day more—in order to settle the dead man's affairs at the home that was now made more desolate than before, and then to depart from it, in all probability for ever. On that day he had been persuaded, though with difficulty, to dine with the Adairs at the *Welcome,* and Jack himself, lest some excuse should be sent by him at the last, walked over to the Hall to fetch him. Their path lay by the river-side, past the lock itself, and through a hundred scenes which were redolent of Arthur's palmy days of youth and love; but he kept his eyes fixed upon the ground in silence, as a mourner follows a bier. Jack attempted no word of comfort or consolation; but when that dreary walk was done, and the well-remembered inn was reached, said—"We have the Blue Parlour, Arthur. Will you wait in there a moment while I speak a word with Blanche in her room ?"

Jack entered the chamber, and, closing the door behind him, found his wife awaiting him with a white and anxious face.

"I have done it," whispered she, in great agitation. "She is there alone."

"And I have sent him in," answered her husband, gravely. Then the two stood and listened with straining ears for some sound from the Blue Parlour, which was almost contiguous to where they were. There broke from it one low, passionate cry, which was succeeded by blank silence. Was that she or he? Was it the wail of measureless woe, or the cry of hushed delight? Minutes passed by that seemed hours.

"Oh, Jack, what can have happened? Heaven knows I did it for the best. But what if the sudden shock has been too much for him!"

"Hush, hush! I hear a woman's sob; that is a good sign. Women always cry when they are very happy."

Without attempting to combat this cynical observation—though, indeed, he who made it had neither the look nor the tone of a cynic—"Come with me, Jack," cried Blanche, impetuously. Her curiosity was overwhelming, but she could not yet restrain her fears. They went out together into the passage. It was she who knocked at the Blue Parlour door, but when there was no answer, it was Jack who opened it. Arthur was sitting on the sofa by the side of Jenny Wren, and with his arm around her waist; he was gray and thin, of course, as before, yet so bright was his smile that he looked already as though he had won back ten years of his lost youth. Jenny was neither gray nor thin, and looked charming; her face, of late grown very pale and thoughtful, wore a little flush upon it that made it simply perfection; even when these intruders entered, her glorious eyes, made soft with tears, turned not towards them, but remained fixed on Arthur.

"Jack," exclaimed he, rising with outstretched hands, "this is your doing, I know. God bless you for it!"

"Nay, my dear friend; it was a joint stratagem of mine and Blanche's. Indeed, she was the chief conspirator; so—if you have a kiss to spare—kiss her; she's waiting for it."

CHAPTER IV.

AN OLD STORY RETOLD.

IN spite of Jack's disclaimer, it was, in fact, chiefly owing to himself that that unlooked-for meeting between Arthur and Jenny had been brought about, although he had been ably seconded by Blanche. She had renewed acquaintance with Alice Renn, after long years of intermission, in one of their river expeditions, and had been surprised to find what a ladylike as well as sensible girl she was. They had known one another as children, when the difference of social rank is not much marked ; but on

her later visits to Swansdale, Blanche had
naturally seen but little of the inn-keeper's
daughter, and what she had heard (although
it was nothing but good) had not prepos-
sessed her in her favour. Her pride had
resented the notion of there being "anything between Arthur and a girl in Jenny's
position ;" and even when her cousin went
abroad, she did not forgive the innocent
object of his attachment. Of late, she had
been still more prejudiced against her, for
it had reached her ears that she had been
the principal cause of quarrel between
Helen and Arthur. It was true that Jack
himself defended Jenny in the matter, but
the advocacy of a husband in such cases
is not always advantageous for the object of
his vindication, and Blanche had come down
to Swansdale, Jenny's foe. That the edge
of her wrath had been in the first place
turned away was owing to Mr. Glyddon, of
whom she had a high opinion, and whose
unstinted praise of the girl awoke in her no
suspicion of his own regard for the village

beauty ; what was unbecoming in the squire, would have seemed to her absolutely disreputable in the rector, and her respect for the cloth precluded any such idea.

In sober fact, however, Mr. Glyddon's encomiums upon Jenny were quite independent of his affection for her. The knowledge of the part she had played with respect to the late Mrs. Tyndall—and the silence she continued to keep concerning the latter's behaviour to her, even now when Helen was no more—filled the rector with admiration ; so that on the very point on which Blanche interrogated him — namely, as to the relations between Jenny and Helen—he spoke with such an enthusiasm of the former's conduct as carried conviction with it. Blanche not only acknowledged to herself that she had been wrong in attributing blame to the lockkeeper's daughter, but sought an early opportunity—which Jack was eager enough to offer—to make reparation to her by graciously renewing their old acquaintance ;

and once brought face to face with one another, the two young women were much too sensible not to acknowledge each other's merits.   The surprise, however, at finding her former playmate what she was, was, of course, on the side of Blanche.   There was nothing unexpected in the grace and elegance of Mrs. Adair, nor, to Jenny, who was of course unacquainted with the failings of fashionable society, even in her naturalness and geniality ; but to Blanche the other seemed a marvel.   That she was beautiful, and delicately so, was nature's doing ; that she was well informed upon subjects not generally within a woman's grasp, as well as upon ordinary topics, was doubtless due to her own diligence ; but that one who had passed her girlhood at an inn, and who was now in a hardly less elevating, and even a more humble condition of life, should possess that ease of manner, joined with the most perfect propriety, which distinguished Jenny, was little short of a miracle.   The drawback of a parent like old Jacob did not strike Blanche so forcibly, because her own father had been himself what Mr. Paul Jones would have termed "no sweatmeat;" but there was enough, and more than enough, in Jenny's superiority to the circumstances in which she was placed, to excite her warmest admiration.

" Whenever I look upon that girl," said Blanche, when with her husband and Mr. Glyddon, " I can't help thinking of that line, ' And beauty born of murmuring sound shall pass into her face.' "

" Perhaps it's the lasher that does it," observed Jack, to whom the poetic description was a little obscure.

" Nay, it *is* the lasher," exclaimed the rector vehemently, carried away for the moment by the recollections evoked by that word, of Jenny's magnanimity and goodness, which did indeed make her fairer in his eyes; " that is, I mean," he added, in some confusion, " the sweet sounds and fair sights which have always

surrounded her from her birth, have doubtless had no inconsiderable share in making
her what she is."

"And yet I have known young ladies
who live by the river-side," said Jack, "at
Wapping and Greenwich, for instance——"

"You ought not to have known them,
sir," broke in Blanche, attacking him vigor-
ously with her parasol.

"Strike, but hear!" exclaimed the victim.
"If you will but hear me out, you will see
that you have no reason for this violence.
I was going to say that in their case I did
not remark that ' beauty born of murmuring
sound ' *did* pass into their face."

"My husband has no poetry in his soul,"
explained Blanche, in apology, to the rector.
" He thinks Alice Renn is just good-look-
ing, and that's all."

The fact was that sagacious Jack had
received his wife's commendations of
Jenny's beauty and merits with studied
coolness. He had found out his previous
mistake in defending her against Blanche's

insinuations, and had now nothing to say for her beyond a few words of tepid praise; but he gave her every opportunity that lay in his power of making her own way into his wife's good graces; and she had completely captivated her. Many an afternoon did the two young women spend with one another, sketch-book in hand, under the lime-tree, and once Blanche had said, though not without some misgiving on the other's account; "Won't you come back in the boat, Jenny, and dine with us at the *Welcome?*"

And Jenny, without a trace of embarrassment, had gladly accepted the invitation. "I should like it of all things," said she; "I have not been in the old place for years."

It was after that dinner that Blanche had observed to her husband : "Upon my word, my dear, I no longer wonder at Arthur's old *tendresse* for that charming girl. Whatever may have been her bringing up, she is every inch a lady : if one met her in a London drawing-room, I am much mistaken if one would not pick her out as *the* most thoroughly self-possessed and well-mannered——"

" My darling, you can't expect *me* to say that," interrupted Jack judiciously.

" No ; but seriously, dear, don't you think so ?"

" She is quite a lady, no doubt, *in mind*," observed the designing one, with just sufficient of detraction in his tone to insure a reply from the Defence.

" Well, but, after all, that is the chief thing," said Blanche. " And really, now poor dear Helen is dead and gone, don't you think Arthur might do worse, if he really feels a warm regard for Jenny, and taking into consideration, of course, the dreadful state in which he is in——"

" But think of old Jacob, and the inn, and the lock," put in Jack.

" Well, of course, all that is bad ; but it's a question of life or death almost to Arthur ; and if he could be rescued from his solitude and melancholy by such a step, I do honestly think that a marriage with Jenny would be the best thing for him."

" Perhaps so," said Jack ; "indeed, my dear, I am pretty sure you are right ; but, unfortunately, there is no getting him over to England."

" That's true," said Blanche, the match-making instincts that belong more or less to every newly married woman, now thoroughly aroused ; " but couldn't we take Jenny abroad with us in the autumn, and throw them together ?"

As this was precisely the plan to which Jack had been leading up to from the very first, and the germ of which had caused him to suggest their trip to Swansdale, he began, after true Machiavelian fashion, to manufacture little obstacles to the idea, for his wife to dispose of, until she was thoroughly set upon carrying it out. In the meantime, however, as we know, circumstances had brought Arthur home, and an opportunity thus offered itself of carrying their scheme at once into operation. It was necessary, indeed, to precipitate proceedings, since, while Uncle Magus lay dead, it would not have been decent to talk of marriage, and now that he was buried, it was Arthur's fixed intention to leave England, probably for ever, in a few hours. But the very urgency of the case put Blanche upon her mettle, and so cunningly did she contrive matters, that Jenny was sitting in the parlour at the *Welcome*, not, indeed, without a thought of Arthur, for her heart was heavy within her at the news she had heard of his altered looks and proposed exile, but without the faintest expectation of seeing him, when a step that she would have known among a thousand startled her from her sad reflections, and made her true heart bound within her.

"Arthur!" cried she, at the sight of him, and a plaintive wail, like the note of an Æolian harp, welled from her lips.

"Jenny!" whispered he, astonishment

and delight overmastering him. " Dear Jenny, can this be true ?"

The poor fellow had thought himself doomed never to see a happy moment again, and was half afraid that he was dreaming.

The suddenness and marvel of their meeting brought that about at once which it might have taken weeks of consideration and probation to have accomplished. These two did not do much credit to the good cheer of the *Welcome,* but sitting on oppo- site sides of the little table, feasted on one another with their eyes ; they did not speak much, but they had to endure some good- natured raillery from their hostess ; for Blanche was in the highest spirits at the success which had crowned her stratagem ; and it was easy to see, by the twinkle in Jack's eyes, that he did not disapprove of her sallies.

" I suppose we shall not see you again, Cousin Arthur, after to-night ?" said she, without a dimple about her mouth, and with the concentrated gravity of the bench of bishops.

"Not see me! Why not?" asked Arthur in astonishment, for he felt a new man: the ideas that he had so seriously entertained a few hours ago had vanished, or, rather, were exchanged for another set entirely different. "Of course you will see us to-morrow." (He had even already put himself in the plural.)

"I thought you meant to go to Liverpool to-morrow," said Blanche demurely, "and start from thence to some tropical region."

"Jack," said Arthur appealingly, "I throw myself on your protection."

"My dear fellow," replied Jack, "I wish I had it to offer you; but I dare not say my soul is my own."

They were all happy enough to take pleasure in the simplest mirth; but the most agreeable spectacle which the evening afforded was the matronly patronage which Blanche, a six months' wife, suddenly began to bestow upon Jenny in her new position; the advice she gave her to the end that she might in future control and subjugate Arthur, and the many wise reflections she let fall concerning the Art and Practice of Married Life. These didactic remarks suffered nothing in their general effect from the retirement of the ladies, for, since it was clearly out of the question to separate Arthur from Jenny, and also would have been a little too marked and significant to leave them alone together, the party did not disunite until it was time to break up. Then "Would you mind seeing Jenny home, Arthur?" asked the hostess with mischievous demureness; "because, if so, we can easily send somebody from the inn." But Arthur did not "mind;" and under the still moonlight, the resoldered pair set out along the well-remembered path, and renewed after that long desuetude their olden talk. They stopped at starting beneath the very tree under which they had parted seven years ago, and kissed again;

every field recalled some fond recollection
of those bygone days, once more so strangely
renovated ; and all the way the river sang
beside them its old song.   Their talk was
of the past alone ; their very kisses smacked
of the halcyon days of youth and of first
love.   Of the intervening time—of Arthur's
exile and his marriage, and of those last
twelve months of widowerhood—not a word
was said ; but the remembrance of it all
was deep within them both, and bore this
fruit of purpose, that there was to be no
more delay.   They had been parted long
enough, they had suffered (no matter through
whose error) long enough, and such separa-
tion and sorrow were to be no more.
Arthur pressed for their immediate union ;
and though Jenny pleaded the nearness of
his uncle Magus' death, as demanding a few
months' postponement of their wedding, six
weeks was the longest limit his patience
would endure.

It is a beautiful provision of nature that
country neighbourhoods are supplied com-

pensatorily with news by rumour, with at
least as great rapidity as the electric wire
can furnish it to the town ; and by break-
fast-time next morning it was somehow
patent to all Swansdale that the young
widower at the Hall was engaged to Jenny
Wren. Such advantage, indeed, has the
tongue over the telegraph, that some circumstances were even enumerated in connection with the event that were absolutely
unknown to the parties themselves. For
example, the squire had meant to marry Jenny
from the moment of his late wife's death,
and had come down to Swansdale to propose to her, immediately that that year and
day had expired which custom has assigned
as the period of marital inconsolability :
again, the squire had resolved *not* to marry
Jenny, and, fearful of her influence over him,
had avoided Swansdale until his uncle's
death had compelled his presence there
when he had at once fallen a victim to her
and so fulfilled his own foreboding : again,
it was Uncle Magus' dying words which

had brought about this happy issue, for seeing how solitary and wretched Arthur was, he had besought him to wed his first love as a remedy for regret for his second : and again, it was only for Uncle Magus' death that Arthur had waited even the very moderate time he had, since, while he was alive, he had hesitated to bring that relative's gray hairs with sorrow to the grave by the commission of such a *mésalliance.*

The second marriage of the young squire of Swansdale afforded, in fact, a topic of conversation for the whole interval between the first rumour of it and the ceremony itself, not only to Swansdale, but to the entire country-side. " The county " disapproved, of course—there is no crime, except, perhaps, rick-burning, which " the county " does disapprove of so much as of a *mésalliance* —but it was intensely interested, nevertheless. Ancient justices of the peace, who had not had oar in hand for twenty years, took to boating again, in order that they might have an excuse for visiting Swansdale Lock,

and seeing the new toast of the Thames—
in which, however, they were doomed to
disappointment, for the Adairs had taken
Jenny back with them to town, whither
Arthur had followed her. Blanche would
have fought the battle for her with "the
county" tooth and nail, but "the county"
was not to be fought. If such and such
were Mrs. Adair's views upon the matter, it
begged to differ from them; that was all *it*
had to say—with the exception of the expression of its thanks to Providence that it
did so differ. In its own drawing-rooms
and in its own particular circles, convention
had not two opinions on this discreditable
affair. In them Arthur Tyndall was charged
with many a high crime and misdemeanour,
such as "setting open flood-gates," "de-
stroying social barriers," "flying in the face
of public opinion," and was finally pronounced to have "lost the respect of all
persons whose respect was worth having,"
and to have "done for himself irreme-
diably."

Blissfully unconscious of having committed these atrocities, or audaciously defiant of the punishment they had entailed upon him, Arthur continued to prosecute his addresses with ardour, for which every opportunity was afforded him. Perhaps the opposition that had been offered to her own engagement made her more favourable than it otherwise would have been, but certainly never had love-match a stancher advocate than was found in Blanche Adair. She even undertook the colossal task of reconciling her mother to the *mésalliance*, though, it must be owned, not with great success. Good and wise as Mrs. Ralph Tyndall was, she had her own traditions, and clung to them.

"Arthur was old enough," she allowed, however, " to know his own mind, and she had no intention of remonstrating with him ; and as for Alice Renn, she herself had always liked her, though it was true she had never contemplated her as a family connection."

This was not very promising, but Blanche was content with it, because her mother expressed herself willing to see Jenny; and to see her, as her new friend believed, was to be conquered by her. And indeed this came about, though not quite in the manner that Blanche had anticipated. Jenny did not "lay herself out" to conciliate Mrs. Ralph quite so much as was expected of her : she showed gratitude and respect, but made no solicitation of patronage. Moreover, on certain matters of private judgment —small enough of themselves, but things on which women are prone to be impatient of contradiction, and especially by their juniors—she held her own, modestly, but resolutely, against Mrs. Ralph, and thereby won her heart.

"I must allow that your friend Jenny has both principle and character," was that lady's frank admission ; and having thus gained a place in her respect, Jenny was not long in securing one in her affections. But the most remarkable feat that this

young woman accomplished was the win-
ning over Mrs. Somers, in whom, as was
to be expected, she found at first her most
strenuous adversary.   She had even refused to meet Jenny, and when she did
come across her, by sheer accident, under
Mrs. Tyndall's roof, had behaved to her
with great scorn and cruelty.   It was only
natural that she should have regarded with
disfavour the girl who had so soon been
chosen the successor of her dead daughter,
but she had no right to treat her (as I am
afraid she called her) as " the dirt under
her feet."   The manners of excellent Mrs.
Somers, in fact, so far from having the re-
pose that stamps the caste of Vere de Vere
on that occasion, were so coarse and violent
as to shock all beholders ; and Jenny, who
was certainly neither deficient in courage
nor self-respect, had uttered no word of
rejoinder.   Her beautiful face had grown
somewhat paler, and her lip had trembled a
little, but not with rage ; her eyes had not
emitted one spark of indignation against

her antagonist, for whom, indeed, she felt
nothing but pity; and she never told Arthur one word of what had happened.

The fruit of this was borne some days
afterwards in a letter of apology from Mrs.
Somers herself : " I ought to have known
better, Miss Alice," it said. " You are not
to blame for loving Arthur, and my conduct
was shameful. I scarcely know what I did
say, for my blood was up (thinking of my
poor dead darling), but I dare say it was
very bad. Since Blanche tells me you behaved like an angel, I conclude, indeed, that
I must have behaved like the other thing.
She says that she is sure, however, that
you will forgive me. One thing, pray, believe, that if I was in a passion, I didn't
give myself airs. As to your being an
innkeeper's daughter (of which they make
so much), I think nothing of that ; my own
husband, though no publican, dealt in hops
himself, which is something like it. . . .
May you be happy, young woman, and
make Arthur so, is my earnest wish." As

to the rest of London society, it was of
small consequence to Jenny whether she
pleased or not, yet, for Arthur's sake, she
strove to please, and succeeded.   The town
often welcomes what the country rejects,
and *vice versâ ;* to the former, freshness,
beauty, originality, are always welcome ;
and even when it was whispered that
Miss Alice Renn had emerged from a lock
on the Thames, it only gave a piquancy to
her charms, and earned for her the title
of the Thames Lily and the Fresh-water
Aphrodite.

On many accounts, indeed, Arthur would
have preferred his marriage to have occurred in London; but there would have
seemed a cowardice in such a proceeding,
from which he shrank ashamed, and in due
time it accordingly took place at Swansdale.

Mrs. Ralph and the Adairs came down
to it, but very few of the neighbouring
families were present, and, what was thought
a still worse sign, Mr. Glyddon did not per-

form the ceremony. Only one or two persons were aware of the real reason which prevented his doing so, and his absence was absurdly enough set down to his disapproval of the event on social grounds. Popular as both bride and bridegroom had severally been in the village, their marriage was not regarded with favour: even there, Jenny's elevation was quite as much resented by those of her own class as by her superiors, while the sentiment of Hamlet was indulged in with respect to the haste with which her bridal had followed the funeral of her predecessor. The frown of "the County" she had borne with great philosophy, for the County had never smiled upon her; but this disapproval of her old friends touched her nearly; nor did she derive any satisfaction from the line of defence which old Jacob always adopted for her (but especially after the amontillado), that "as for his daughter Jenny, she might have looked a deal higher, had she chosen, and married a lord" (from Eton) "years ago."

However, these little drawbacks were as nothing in comparison with the bliss she felt in Arthur's love ; and never did a happier or a more lovely bride reply " I will," to the parson's " Wilt thou ? " than Jenny Wren on the day she wedded Arthur Tyndall.   The compensation had come to her at last for those long years of Patience and Disappointment, and surely, surely there was no disaster in Fate's store, save death itself, that *could* shadow those bright days to be !

CHAPTER IV.

TOO MUCH HAPPINESS.

ARTHUR had left it to Jenny to select the spot in which they should pass their honeymoon, premising only (for fear, perhaps, that she might have hit upon the Lakes, where one does not, as a rule, spend honeymoons two years running) that it should be somewhere abroad; and she had chosen Brussels. It was curious to see how astonished, nay, petrified with alarm, he had looked when she made that choice.

" Good Heavens! Why Brussels, Jenny?"

" For no reason, dearest Arthur, save

6—2

that which my own vanity suggested : I knew you had been ill and wretched there, alone, and I flattered myself that you would now feel differently, and perhaps ascribe the change to me."

Of course, this explanation was eminently satisfactory ; and as Jenny added that she was but an ignoramus, to whom everything on the continent would have the charm of novelty, Arthur proposed Italy. So to Florence, Rome, and Naples they journeyed, and a very happy time it was to both of them. To Jenny it was a new world of beauty, for she had never seen any other landscapes save those homely English river ones (which, after all, however, have no rivals), made up of wood and water and hanging banks ; while the wonders of art were almost as new to her. She enjoyed the immense advantage of seeing these last with a companion who critically knew nothing about them ; who did not rave about this, that, and the other, until she was afraid to have an opinion of her own,

nor chatter the art shibboleth in her ears
till the beauties faded out of the canvas.
She did not say much herself, but what she
did say contrasted very vividly with those
second-hand notes of admiration he had
heard other young ladies utter in similar
circumstances, and gave him even a higher
opinion of her good sense and taste than
he had entertained before ; only, with one
other, he always loyally forbore to put her
in comparison, and of her, Jenny, on her
part, never spoke. She would have liked
to have spoken of her ; and certainly would
have taken care to do so only with tenderness and respect ; but it was not for her to
break the silence which Arthur so rigidly
maintained upon that subject. He never
once mentioned Helen's name, or in the
most distant manner alluded to her, and
this Jenny put down to an over-sensitive-
ness with respect to herself : he had once
discarded her for Helen, and perhaps he
imagined that this was a source of bitterness to her ; and she would have liked to

have had the opportunity of telling him
that this was no longer so ; that she had
never wondered, even when she felt most
forlorn, that a beautiful and accomplished
young woman, such as Helen, who had
evidently also loved him tenderly, should,
after so long an absence, have erased the
memory of her own girlish charms, and
that now, at all events, every feeling of
humiliation was forgotten in the great happiness he had bestowed upon her.

Jenny *was* intensely happy ; and Arthur,
too, seemed to have become quite another
man.   She was often asked, by chance
companions of her own sex, how it was
that her husband looked so old and yet so
young ; so gray and careworn in the face,
and yet so eye-bright and conspicuously
happy.

" It was through an illness that he had
at Brussels," was her reply to all such questions ; but about that illness she knew little
more than they ; nothing, in fact, save
what Blanche had told her ; for Arthur

had never opened his lips concerning it, and her delicate instinct warned her that there was some reason for his silence; perhaps the time he spent there had been too immediately connected with Helen's death to permit allusion to it. Notwithstanding the dogma that husbands should have no secrets from their wives, complete confidence is hardly to be expected by the young woman who weds a widower; and Jenny was much too sensible to be exacting. She was a perfect Griselda, indeed, in this respect, and the very antipodes of Helen : some people may say that that only became her, considering the position from which her lord and master had raised her; and certainly, in a sense, it *did* become her ; but if such concession be the usual consequence of marrying beneath one, men would surely never be so foolish as to wed in their own sphere. Moreover, as to money, although it is true Helen had been an heiress, Jenny, for her part, thanks to old Jacob's frugality, was by no means portionless,

and, indeed, had brought quite as much to
Arthur as he possessed himself. As one
example among many in the difference between her and her predecessor with respect
to the possession of " a will of their own,"
we may instance this : that when, after a
few weeks of unclouded sunshine, both
within and without, Arthur hinted at their
return to Swansdale, Jenny at once acceded
to it. The idea could scarcely have been
very welcome to her. Abroad, she had
been everywhere admired and caressed ;
while, at home, she had only to expect—at
all events, until time should wear away the
prejudice of her neighbours—cold looks,
cold shoulders, and unjust suspicions.
Still, Swansdale was to be her home, and
above all, Arthur's home ; and she did not
ask for a day's delay. It would have
seemed to her as unjustifiable to do so, as
for a public schoolboy, whose vacation is
over, to demand another week of holiday
without any reasonable excuse—such as an
increase of the royal family.

The Tyndalls, therefore, returned to Swansdale. It was fortunate that the difference of their reception, as compared with that which they had accorded Arthur and his first wife, did not, of course, strike Jenny. No bells were rung, no rector met them at the station ; no triumphal arch was raised for them to pass beneath it. The school, however, had assembled at the gates, as on the last occasion, but of their own accord, and out of love for their old teacher, and gave Jenny a welcome that brought happy tears into her eyes. The servants, too, now not so numerous as of yore, lined the hall as they entered, to do honour to their new mistress; but Mrs. Glyn's manner was even stiffer than her silk gown. She could not forget that long ago, as it was, there had been a time when Miss Alice Renn had been content to take a cup of tea with her in the housekeeper's room, and had not dreamed of aspiring to the drawing-room ; while the butler was filled with dread imaginings of the day

when he should have to " demean hisself"
by waiting on old Jacob at his son-in-law's
table, and helping him to sherry.

" There'll be deuced little left of our fine
West India Brown," was his dark foreboding, " if that old lushington gets the
run of our cellar."

This apprehension, however, was, as it
turned out, quite groundless ; for, in the
first place, West India Brown was an
article always stigmatised by the adorer of
amontillado as " treacley stuff ;" and, in the
second, Jacob Renn was much too " independent," after his own fashion, " to come
anywhere where he might not be welcome ;
though (mind you !), for the matter of that,
he had been in company in his time with
the best in the land, and knew how to be-
have himself (thank Heaven !), whether it
was to a dook or a dustman. If his gal
wanted to see her old father, she might
come down as often as she pleased to the
lock, and, for the matter of that, the squire
with her—why not ?—and take a dish of

tea." And this judicious compromise was, in fact, effected. Matters generally settled down much better than might have been expected ; and every day saw the waves of opposition growing smoother and smoother, for, in quiet, conciliating Mrs. Tyndall, they had nothing to break against. Her only real trouble, in short, was, that the rector could not be persuaded to visit at the Hall : it was painful enough to him, poor fellow, to have to look upon her and Arthur in their pew on Sunday, from the too commanding elevation of his pulpit. But, during their absence, he had done them the good turn to thoroughly disabuse the mind of "the county" as to the reason for his holding aloof from them. Some feeble female, at a dinner-party, had ventured to congratulate Mr. Glyddon upon the stand he had made against "unequal matches"—meaning the tacit opposition he was supposed to have afforded to Jenny's marriage, by deputing its solemnisation to another—and his reply had astonished the company not a little.

"Whoever had married Miss Alice Renn," said he—" and I speak of all men without exception, with whom I have ever been acquainted—must needs, in so doing, have made an unequal match, for none are worthy of her."

" Well, upon my word!" ejaculated the feeble female. " You do astonish me."

" Nevertheless, madam," returned the rector, " I assure you, upon my word of honour, that what I have said is true."

These words, which circulated from dinner-table to dinner-table, were by no means without their influence, for Mr. Glyddon was known not to be one to "say things" with a mere view to astonish, and the effect was seen in many "a call" at Swansdale Hall, which, though it may have had curiosity for its motive, in the first instance, bore good social fruit; those who came as critics returned again and again in a much more kindly spirit; and one or two of the more sagacious even confessed to themselves that, so far from being what they had ex-

pected to find her, the second Mrs. Tyndall was "perfectly charming." At all
events, they professed themselves to be
Jenny's friends, and though she did not
need them for herself, for she was one of
those women who are never idle, or find
time heavy on their hands for want of such
companionship, she welcomed them gladly
for her husband's sake. It was a satisfaction to her to think, not that he need no
longer be ashamed of his wife as one "sent
to Coventry" by her neighbours (for that
she knew he could never be), but that other
people could no longer attribute to him
such a feeling. Nay, Jenny Wren was but
a woman after all (though none the less
charming for that restriction), and it doubtless gratified her, when she went out to
dine with her great neighbours, to know
that she came beyond (or perhaps disap-
pointed) their expectations of her. It had
been supposed, at first, that she would have
a difficulty in restraining her knife from
visiting her mouth, and in extending her

conversation beyond the topic of the coal-
traffic on the Thames; and yet not six
months had elapsed before this "young
person" had advanced to such social pre-
ferment, that Lady Trottermout, the member's wife, had graciously pronounced her
"quite an acquisition!"

All this, however, was but a very small
item in the great sum of Jenny's happiness.
Every day seemed to draw her husband
nearer to her heart, and her to his; while
supremely content as she felt in her present
lot, the future had now in store for her even
a still greater bliss—the gift of offspring.

"Oh, my darling," whispered she to Arthur, when she first told him of it, "I feel
so very, very happy that it gives me fear.
The day of my life seems almost too bright
to keep its blue."

"Nay," returned he, with tenderness,
"this is only the compensation which is
owed you for long years of patient sorrow
and (alas) ill-treatment; you will be happier and happier every day, believe me, till

the time comes—and may it be long distant, is my selfish prayer—for you to become an angel ; so happy, that the change
at last from earth to heaven will not be no-
ticeable ; nay, it seems to me that it will be
no change at all, darling, since in my eyes
you are an angel already."

It was very pleasant to her to hear him
use such loving hyperboles, and still more
pleasant to see him so hopeful and happy,
who, but six months before, had seemed to
have neither hope nor happiness within
him, for to what could that change be
owing save to their mutual love ! He was
going out to shoot that day over a neighbour's preserves ; and while left alone at
home, she repeated over and over again to
herself those tender words, and called up
the bright look with which they had been
accompanied, to gild his absence. It was
a dull November day, with occasional
showers of sleet, and, as she was not likely
to be troubled with visitors, she resolved
to give it up to " setting things to rights "

in her little boudoir. This room was full
of knick-knacks, which (such things not
being much in her line) she had never
thoroughly investigated and explored,
though, to some women, it would have
been a great delight to do so. Her predecessor, for example, "doted" on inlaid
cabinets, old china, and Indian rarities in
ivory and sandal-wood, and had surrounded
herself with them in her bower. The
knowledge that they had been Helen's,
might perhaps have given Jenny even less
of interest in them than she would have
otherwise felt; but if so, she was unaware
of any such feeling; it was with no other
sensation than that of a somewhat feeble
curiosity that she proceeded to examine
these treasures.

A Japanese cabinet, as being the most
considerable object in the room, first engaged her attention. It was in construc-
tion simple enough, and, indeed, almost the
fac-simile of that in Arthur's smoking-
room, except that where his books stood

there were here pigeon-holes, and that
what were pigeon-holes in his cabinet were
here little painted drawers, each with a tag
of silver by which to pull them out. Both
articles of furniture served the purposes of
a desk, and the late Mrs. Tyndall had
habitually made use of this one for her
somewhat dainty letter-writing. House-
keeping and accounts she had left entirely
to Mrs. Glyn, but what correspondence she
had carried on with old school-friends,
breathing eternal attachment, or with her
more recent acquaintances in the neighbourhood—" requesting the favour of, &c.,
&c." or " accepting with pleasure, &c. &c."
—had been transacted here, with little
people in ebony and silver disporting themselves on every drawer above her, and ex-
pressing, by inappropriate acrobatic action,
their sympathy with the difficulties of com-
position.

Jenny was not aware of this, and
it gave her a momentary feeling of dis-

comfort, upon opening the desk, to find
the blotting-book lying before her just as it
had been left there two years ago—with
"Helen Tyndall" in reverse imprinted
on it—probably from the last note which
her predecessor had ever penned. With
that exception, everything wore the appearance of having been looked to and
set in order much more recently. Every
scrap of note-paper, for instance, which
had borne the dead woman's monogram
had been carefully removed, and it was
with the assurance that she would come
upon no private record likely to give
pain to herself or others that Jenny
continued her investigations. Great was
her surprise, then, to find in the first
long drawer—the one most likely to be
opened by any one who used the desk,
and the one most certain not to be passed
over by the person, whoever it was, that
had set the cabinet in order—a large envelope with this address :

" To be opened by the first person who shall chance to find it after my death.

(Signed)

" HELEN TYNDALL."

CHAPTER VI.

ITH a beating heart, and a mind presaging she knew not what of evil, Jenny broke the envelope and seal (a large one with the Tyndall crest upon it, the die of which she had seen in the library), and read as follows :

"I, Helen Tyndall, being in sound health of mind, though sorely troubled and distressed therein, hereby do make confession, that on the 24th day of November last, being with Alice Renn on the wooden

bridge above the lasher, near her house, I
did maliciously push her into the river,
being incited thereto by hate and jealousy
—and this is the truth, whatever this girl
may choose to say to the contrary, out of
pretended tenderness for my memory, and
to suit her own ends. Moreover, I hereby
solemnly declare that I do go in fear of my
life from my husband, Arthur Tyndall, who
loves me not, but is bent on my death, in
order that he may marry the girl aforesaid ;
and I charge whosoever shall find this
paper, to make strict inquiry into the cause
of whatsoever death I shall have died :
whether by sudden seizure of disease (as it
may have appeared), or by (seeming) accident, such as the being thrown out of a
carriage, or drowning (with both which he
has menaced me), so that the guilt may be
brought home where it is due.

"Swansdale Hall, December 31, 1860."

Jenny rose, staggered to the door, and
locked it ; then dropped into her chair to

think—if the passing through her brain of a score of weird and hideous speculations could be termed *thinking*.

" And but two hours ago," muttered she, with that self-mocking smile which is Despair's forlornest wear, " he told me that I should be even happier than I was!" Shocked and horrified as she was, however, her natural good sense, even in that extremity, soon rallied itself, and led her from the contemplation of her own wretchedness to examine the grounds on which it had arisen.   She had hardly any doubt in her own mind that Helen had written the document that lay before her ; it was scarce humanly possible that so base and wicked a trick could have been played upon her by another ; but still there *was* a doubt, and she hastened to resolve it.   The late Mrs. Tyndall's handwriting was not familiar to her ; but in the music-stand in that very room, close to the small seraphine on which she had been wont to play, were several books that had belonged to her predecessor, and perhaps one of them would have her name written on its fly-leaf. She opened one—the oldest of them, as it happened, and just within it were the words, "Helen Somers, from her dear Mamma, March 18, 1854." That must have been when Helen was quite a girl, and yet the handwriting corresponded nearly with that of the document; still it was possible that her mother might have written the words. Jenny opened another : "Helen Tyndall, August, 1860," and compared it with the "Helen Tyndall, December 31, 1860." There could be no longer any doubt : the autographs were identical.

Two years ago, then, or twenty-three months exactly, just after she had recovered from her last illness, from the effects of which she was still suffering when she went abroad, Helen had written that terrible statement with her own hand; and she had perished leaving the lie behind her, in hopes to blacken her husband's memory ! Not for one instant did Jenny believe that

the thing was true, and yet it made her
scarcely less wretched than if she had
believed it. For what an extremity of
desperation and malignancy must have
possessed this woman, to write such a
document upon the *chance* that some such
catastrophe might happen as actually did
occur !

"Or by (seeming) accident, such as the
being thrown out of a carriage."

Jenny's blood ran cold as she reperused
these words, at the idea of how easily this
infamous document might have fallen into
other hands and *been believed.* Nay, how
was it that it had escaped that mischance ?
How was it possible that Mrs. Glyn, or
whoever else had set that cabinet in order
for her own use (as had evidently been
done), could have omitted to see it, lying
as it did in the most obvious place, with
the exception of the open desk itself, that it
could lie ? Or, again, was it possible that
Mrs. Glyn had found it, read it, and sealed
it up again, in order that it might meet the

very eyes which had just perused it ? The
house-keeper had always held herself stiffly
—almost antagonistically—with respect to
her : and certainly, if she had become
acquainted with this terrible statement
(wherein her new mistress was, in fact, distinctly designated as the cause of her predecessor's untimely end), it was no wonder.
But, on the other hand, the housekeeper's
dislike of Jenny had by no means been so
marked that it could be set down to a cause
that might well have justified even loathing,
and, moreover, it had of late months very
sensibly mitigated, which it surely would
not have done under the circumstances supposed. What was not the least remarkable
in this strange and shocking document, was
its mixture of truth and falsehood ; the unnecessary confession of the writer's own
offence against Jenny in conjunction with
the slanderous accusation brought against
Arthur. What need had there been for
Helen to accuse herself at all ? On reflection, however, Jenny concluded that this

had been done to make the *vraisemblance*
of the false charge more striking.   Helen
knew that she would be dead before the
document was discovered—or "chanced"
it (and it was this "chancing" so many
things that was one of the most dreadful
features of the case, as evidencing her utter
desperation)—and had therefore cared not
what should be said against herself, if only
she could disgrace and harm him of whom
she was so frantically and unjustly jealous;
while the very fact of her confessing so
solemnly to such a crime would give a
plausibility to the rest of her statement;
and, moreover, she could not be sure that
Jenny herself would not reveal what had
happened at the lasher, even if she had not
already done so.   Finally, the motive of
the whole proceeding seemed only too
clear : either to prevent Arthur's marriage
with herself (Jenny) ; or, if it had taken
place, then to render them both wretched.

And with one, at least, it had succeeded.
In spite of her confidence in her husband's

innocence, and of the indignant flush which her absorbing love for him called up when the shadow of a suspicion of his guilt came across her mind, yet at times it would cross it. The poison of Suggestion stole into her being despite all opposition, or even, perhaps, assisted by it, for, with every struggle, the hateful presumption seemed to grow more specious.

"Suppose," at last she found herself saying, "that this is *true*"—and in an instant, without, as it seemed, volition of her own, she was standing on the hearth-rug, holding the envelope with its contents above the flame; but the next moment she turned away, with a "No; I will not. If it could be true—if it were possible to believe that Arthur could be guilty, I would have burned this thing, lest it should harm him; but knowing that he is as innocent of crime as the child I bear within me, I keep it. It may do its worst."

This revelation of her own faith in her husband comforted her for a little; but as she sat pondering whether to tell him, or not, of what she had discovered, again she found herself on the old track of thought. She was still free from doubt of Arthur, or flattered herself that she was so ; but putting the supposititious case of another having found this paper who had her own lights to guide him to a conclusion, she was compelled to confess that it was only too likely to be an adverse one. For why had her husband never so much as opened his lips concerning his late wife, unless they had been sealed by some secret known to himself alone ? And why had his frame shrunk to a skeleton, and his hair turned gray within a few months of her decease, unless remorse had withered the one and bleached the other ? Assumed it was *not* remorse—which, for her own part, she took for granted—yet there must be some motive for such reticence; and his disinclination to enter upon the subject had, at all events, this effect, that she resolved to keep her present discovery to herself.

Her first proceeding was to satisfy her-

self that it was her own to keep—that it
was not already shared by another. With
this intent, she rang her bell, and desired
the maid to send Mrs. Glyn to the boudoir.
The housekeeper came, respectful, quiet,
unconciliating, without any symptom of such
embarrassment as might have been looked
for had she been in expectation of the event
that had just occurred. The summons was
unusual ; for Jenny, accustomed to wait
upon herself, rarely required the services
even of her maid ; and there was just a
touch of surprise in the woman's inquiry as
to what her mistress might be pleased to
want, and that was all.

" I want your advice, Mrs. Glynn, as to a
new distribution of the furniture here : the
arrangement does not quite please me.
This cabinet, for instance, as it strikes me,
is too close to the fire-place."

" Possibly, madam. The late Mrs. Tyndall used it as her desk, which caused it to
be placed in that position. Perhaps it
should stand nearer the window."

" That is just what I was thinking, Mrs. Glyn.   Here, for instance.   Would you mind helping me to push it there, and to put this reading-table in its place?— Thanks."

Other little alterations were made ; and then Jenny remarked how beautifully clean and thoroughly in order everything had been kept.

" I am glad you are pleased, madam," was the housekeeper's stiff rejoinder : it did not please her to be praised for such a simple act of duty.

" Did you take all this trouble with your own hands, Mrs. Glyn ?"

" Certainly, madam.   I cleaned out every drawer myself.   It was not for a servant— that is, an *under*-servant," added the old lady proudly, "to be peeping and prying into cabinets and such-like, where, for all I knew, my late mistress might have left things of a private nature."

Jenny felt cold to her very heart : the old lady spoke with such significance, and almost severity, that she began to fear the worst. She was determined, however, to know it, if it was so, and not, at least, to suffer from suspense.

"And *did* you find anything of that nature?" inquired she, boldly.

"No, madam," replied the old lady, more stiffly than ever, and with a what-is-that-to-you? expression of countenance. "If I had done so, it would, of course, have been my duty to inform my master of the circumstance."

"True," said Jenny thoughtfully. She was far too deeply interested in the matter in hand to be annoyed by the other's manner; her mind was occupied by the alternatives of the case. If this woman was speaking the truth—and she had little doubt but that she was—the document must have been found elsewhere by somebody else, and placed, after the "putting to rights" had been effected, in the spot where she had found it. Of course, this might have been done by some servant of the

house ; but that seemed in the highest
degree improbable. As to Jenny's own
maid, Susan—a most excellent girl, but a
persistent chatterbox—her mistress felt convinced that, had she become possessed of
such a secret, she could not have kept it to
herself for four-and-twenty hours.

"No one but Susan has access to the
boudoir, I believe, Mrs. Glyn?"

"Certainly not, madam : and after my
late mistress's death, and until you came"—
there was an ungraciousness about those
last three words that amounted to down-
right incivility — "the room was always
locked, and the key kept in my possession.
I sincerely trust that nothing is a-missing :
nothing ever *has* been a-missing——"

"Nor is likely to be while you are here,
Mrs. Glyn," interrupted Jenny gently.
"You must not be angry with me, my good
friend, if I ask you one question more."

The soft answer turned away the housekeeper's wrath, and made her sensible of
the impropriety of her manner. "Angry,

madam ? I hope not. It would be very wrong in me, as well as out of my place, to be so ; but I was annoyed lest something should have been lost."

" Nothing has been lost ; but yet I wish to ask you whether, to your knowledge, this room has been entered since the late Mrs. Tyndall's death by any one but Susan and yourself ?"

" By no one, madam.—Stay," added the housekeeper; "let me be quite correct. There was one old lady, last July, just after your marriage, who asked to see the grounds ; many do so in the summer months ; and my orders were from my master, as from his father before him, always to admit such visitors. After she had seen the garden, she wished to go over the house. I was laid up myself with rheumatism, but one of the girls came to me with the request—I think it was Jane—and I said ' No.' Then the lady sent her back again with her address card, ' Mrs. Montague,' from London, if I remember right—and the message, that

she asked the favour as having been an old
acquaintance of my late mistress ; and then,
of course, I was obliged to give way ; and
Jane went with her over the whole house,
this room included, for I recollect giving
out the key."

" Had you any remembrance of your late
mistress knowing such a person ?"

" No ; I confess I had not, ma'am.   But
then she had many London acquaintances
whom I did not know, and this might very
well have been one of them ; and if so, it
would have been thought very uncivil in
me to have refused permission.   A person
in my position cannot act upon her own re-
sponsibility, you see."

" I quite understand.   You did very
right, Mrs. Glyn ; and there has been no
harm done.   So far as I am concerned,
pray use your own discretion in future concerning visitors, which I am sure will be
always judicious.   But it is your taste I
want just now, as to these chairs and
tables."

So Jenny went on to re-arrange the furniture ; reconciling herself with the old lady
at the same time by accepting her sug-
gestions, until the latter came down from
her pedestal of lofty self-respect, and seemed
quite won over to her new mistress. Jenny
now felt positively certain, first, that the
housekeeper had no knowledge of the
document left by Helen ; and secondly,
that somebody had, or else how could it
have been placed where she had found it ?
That person, whoever it was, probably
knew also the contents of the envelope,
since, otherwise, he (or she) would surely
have opened it (since it was addressed to
the finder), and in so doing have broken
the seal, which bore no trace of re-impres-
sion. This individual, then, must have
been a confidante of Helen's, and intrusted
with the document for the very purpose of
placing it, in case of her death, where it
was sure to meet Jenny's eyes. Jenny's
suspicions naturally fixed themselves on
Mrs. Montague. Later in the day, there-

fore, she took an opportunity of questioning Jane about that personage. The girl well remembered the circumstance of the lady's visit, and of her being shown over the house and boudoir. She was an old lady, gray and somewhat feeble, and wore blue spectacles, to keep the glare from her eyes. She spoke very little, but seemed interested in what she saw. She was staying for a few days, as she understood her to say, at the *Railway Hotel;* and the visit was made late in the month, within a day or two, in fact, of the Tyndalls' return home from the Continent.

The knowledge thus acquired, that there was some living being whom she could challenge and confront concerning this cowardly attack on Arthur, gave Jenny unspeakable satisfaction. This horrible shadow of suspicion, which might have darkened her days for ever, had she had to combat through it with the Dead, might surely now be dissipated; and it should be the object of her life to get this done. It

was hard, however, to control her emotions,
to simulate happiness in her tone, and ease
in her manner, to her husband, when he
came in that day from shooting, and met
her with his accustomed caress. It was
hard to lend a ready ear to his talk at
table, of the birds in "the fouracre" which
had got up wild, yet fallen right and left to
his double barrel, and of the single bird
that had risen at his very feet in the tur-
nips, and got away scot-free. And yet his
very cheerfulness gave her comfort, in the
assurance (needless though it was) that
such wholesome simple thoughts could
never have an abiding-place in a mind that
carried such a burden as had been imputed
to it by the slanderous paper, which she
carried in her bosom—not for love, but
safety, next to the little golden anchor,
which had been restored to her once
more.

In the drawing-room that evening she
cautiously ventured upon the question on
which she had been meditating for hours.

"By-the-by, dear, Mrs. Glyn tells me that when we were away in Italy a visitor called and asked to see the grounds."

"It is likely enough, my darling," answered he, carelessly; "I dare say there were a dozen; and he must have been of a very moderate disposition not to have insisted upon seeing the house also. For, though, goodness knows, there's not much to look at, I've known my poor father—who never refused a request of that kind, however unreasonable—retire from room to room, in order that sightseers should have their will in that respect."

"Oh, but this was not an ordinary sightseer; it was a lady, who said that she was an old acquaintance."

"Indeed! Dear me!" observed he, smiling, "has Mrs. Glyn been making you jealous, Jenny?"

"An acquaintance not of yours, Arthur, but of—of Helen's—a Mrs. Montague."

The smile faded suddenly away from Arthur's features; it was the first time that

Helen's name had been mentioned between them ; he remained quite silent.

" Do you remember the name of Montague ?" inquired Jenny, timidly.

" I have never heard of it. I am nearly sure the person must have been an impostor. Those tourist-people will say anything to gain admittance where they have no business."

The speech was wholly unlike Arthur. There was no exclusiveness about his character : the vile and vulgar notion, held by many persons who pique themselves upon being above the vulgar, of keeping their property within walls, and permitting no eye save their own to refresh itself even on their trees and grassland, was abhorrent to him ; the stranger was always welcome within his gates. His irritation could only be due to her having trespassed upon that ground which he did desire to keep private —the subject of his late wife.

Jenny was very sorry ; sorry to have angered him (for the first time, too, since their marriage); and still more sorry for the cause. But what distressed her most of all was to learn that he had never so much as heard the name of Mrs. Montague. If it turned out to be a feigned one, it was only the more likely that the person who bore it should have been she who placed the document in the cabinet; and it was not likely, having thus accomplished her purpose, that she should reveal who she really was. Henceforth, therefore, Jenny would have to contend with her enemy in the Dark.

CHAPTER VII.

THE reception which Helen's name had met with from her husband, even when thus casually introduced, would have decided Jenny, had her resolve not been already fixed to keep the discovery of that terrible legacy of his late wife from Arthur's eyes, and this weight falling upon her as it did at a time when she was peculiarly ill-fitted to bear such an undivided burden, crushed out of her both health and spirits. In vain Arthur endeavoured to persuade himself that her changed appearance was, as the village doctor assured him, due to her condition only, and that in a few months she would be herself again. Death had of late been too busy about him to permit that feeling of false security into which most men in such cases are so willing to be lulled; he was certain that she was fading and failing, nor could her constant efforts to appear well and cheerful impose upon his anxious mind. To her, of course, he said nothing but what the doctor had said; but he watched her day by day with an aching heart, and at last wrote as follows to his " other self," Jack Adair—who had been recently blessed with a little daughter, to whom he had asked Arthur to stand sponsor—for the counsel that had never failed him yet, and had been wise even when rejected.

" My dearest wife, who will do anything in the world to please me, has seen a physician from town, and he corroborates the opinion expressed by our own doctor— that there is nothing the matter with her save what April next will see the end of.

Heaven grant it may be so, but I cannot flatter myself with any such view. If she had been well enough, nothing would have pleased me better than to have come up with her to see my little god-daughter christened, and, indeed, she pressed me to do so; but I feel she ought not to travel in her present state, and O Jack! I dread to leave her, even for a day, lest, at no distant time, I may have to say to myself, 'I might have lived one day longer with her whom I have lost for ever.' You will say I am morbidly apprehensive about her—that she was always of a good constitution, and that, though Swansdale may not be healthy for everybody, it is her native air. They have said all this to me, and much more, but they have not their all at stake, as I have; and they do not know what I know. To the doctors—to everybody, in fact, she presents a smiling face, a cheerful air, is uncomplaining, and protests that there is nothing amiss with her; and she convinces them. For me, likewise, she puts on her best looks, and chatters—no, she never chatters—converses gaily; but it is plain to me that it is a continual effort with her, and at times, poor soul, she utterly breaks down.   I have seen traces of tears on her sweet face, notwithstanding the pains she takes to hide them, and my Jenny has no cause for tears.   I almost wish she had, that I might put these down to it.   What frightens me most about her, is the terrible rapidity with which this change has set in. Three weeks ago she was looking as well as ever she did—better, to my loving eyes, Jack, than on the day I married her—and as happy as a fairy; to-day she is pale, thin, and dejected.   If the doctors had not positively assured me that it was not the case, I should have said: 'She is in a rapid decline'—that is, I should have thought so, for to have said it, even to you, Jack, feeling that it was so, would have been impossible.   Well, we cannot come to you, you see.   But can you not come to *us?* Will not dear Blanche, for Jenny's sake, bring down her babe for Jenny to fondle (which she longs to do), and spend the first days of the new year—how I tremble to think what it may take away! — at Swansdale ? If you wrote to invite your-selves, that would give my dear wife greater pleasure, while it would prevent her from suspecting that I had told you this sad story. Come, dear friend, and give me your counsel, and, if it please God, your comfort."

The Adairs were people who not only never hesitate about performing a kind action, but who perform it at once. The return of the post brought a letter from Blanche to Jenny, proposing a visit to the Hall as soon as " baby " was pronounced fit to travel ; and a few days saw them at Swansdale.

In the opinion of the new-comers, Ar-thur's fears had greatly exaggerated his wife's indisposition, though they pronounced her far from well : they thought her face somewhat wan and " drawn ;" but " Dear

me, what does Arthur expect?" laughed
the young matron to her husband; "and as
for her spirits, I call them excellent, considering." And though, after the first flush
of their reception, which had really given
Jenny great pleasure, had passed away, and
when the novel duties of hostess were not
compelling her to cheerfulness, they perceived that there really was something
amiss with her, it did not strike them as
very serious. Mrs. Adair, indeed, curiously
enough, thought less of it than her husband;
for where Jenny was happiest was in the
chamber, now dubbed the nursery, with
Blanche and her babe. Even then, indeed,
while Mrs. Tyndall clasped the child in her
arms, or rocked it to sleep upon her knees,
the unbidden tears would sometimes start
into her eyes; but Blanche set that down
to the happiness of an expectant mother —
the thought of the coming treasure of her
own, which a few months would give her.
Jack thought her "somewhat staid" and
"quiet," and "with as few words as a

Quakeress," and though it was true that "girls often altered after marriage," the change was greater than he should have expected in one whose character had been so marked as Jenny ; still he could honestly assure his friend that he saw no ground for alarm.

Adair's surprise was therefore considerable, when, on the Sunday after his arrival, staying behind the rest of the Hall party, after the church service, in order to speak with Mr. Glyddon, that gentleman inquired of him somewhat abruptly, what made Mrs. Tyndall look so ill. " I don't go to the Hall, now, Adair, as you know," said he.

" I wish you would—they all wish you would," put in Jack quickly, but tenderly (for he knew all about that business).

" I wish I *could,*" sighed the rector ; " but let that pass. What I was about to say to you was, that Mrs. Tyndall's looks alarm me. What ails her ?"

" Nothing," said Jack ; " at least the doctors say so ; though Tyndall himself, to tell the truth, is somewhat anxious about her."

" He has cause," said the rector gravely. " Look at me, Adair. We are old friends, and can tell one another the truth and bear to hear it. You see me changed, do you not, from what I was a year ago or less ?"

" Yes ; you are aged by more than the last twelve months. And though you de- serve to be happy, old fellow, if any man ever did, you look——"

"Wretched !" said the rector, quietly finishing the other's sentence. " My looks, old friend, so far do not belie me ; but no matter for that. I wish to speak of Mrs. Tyndall. What you see in me, *I* see in *her*. A month ago (God bless her !), that woman was like a bird, a flower, anything that has beauty, and vigour, and freshness ; the song, the fragrance, were not for me ; but, Heaven knows, I grudged them not to him for whom they were. In my own for- lorn and desolate condition, it was a consolation to me to reflect that she at least was happy."

They were in the vestry; not a sentimental spot, as partaking of the nature of a "green-room," with very commonplace " properties ;" but the poor rector here sat down in it, in his bands and cassock, and sobbed like a child.

" Heaven help you!" ejaculated Jack, greatly dismayed, though touched, by this proceeding, and somewhat in doubt as to the propriety of invoking a blessing on a clergyman. " I'm deuced sorry for you, and all that, upon my soul."

" I know, I know," said the rector. " Pardon me this, old fellow ; I thought I had been stronger. It is the thought of her—of Mrs. Tyndall being in trouble, that moves me so. If she is not ill, Adair, and very ill, she is very wretched. Not as I am, of course, nor for the same reason : you would never have heard me say so, had I thought *that*. Tyndall is kind to her, I know ; but something is killing her. Let

him find out what it is before it is too
late."

"How can you possibly know this?" was
the phrase that rose to Adair's lips, but he
did not utter it.   This man, who loved her,
he reflected, must needs have keener eyes
than he.   Few and small had been the
opportunities by which Glyddon had arrived at the same conclusion to which
Arthur had also come; but their concur-
rence of opinion on such a point struck
Jack as very noteworthy.   He could not
well go to Arthur and tell him what the
rector had said; if he did so, even if it
were taken in good part, it would only increase his friend's apprehensions without
suggesting any remedy; so he resolved
upon a bolder, or, at least, a more direct
course of proceeding.   There was this
difference between Mr. Glyddon's view of
Jenny's case and Arthur's: the latter at-
tributed her ailment, whatever it was, to
physical causes; the former ascribed it to
some distress of mind.   If the rector had

laid this to the account of his successful
rival's behaviour, the idea might have been
set down to jealousy ; but he had expressly
exonerated Arthur from any such charge,
and even pointed him out as the person
most interested in the matter, and to whom
warning was due. It was a *bonâ fide*
opinion, and, so far as it did not impute
disease, chimed in with that of the doctor's.
It was true that Arthur had expressly stated
that his wife had nothing on her mind : it
was only three weeks ago, he had said, that
she had expressed herself as perfectly
happy—" so happy that it made her afraid
for fear something should happen ;" but,
then, even the best of wives did not always
confide everything to their husbands, and
especially if they thought that the confidence
would vex them. True, it was most unlikely that anything of so painful a description as to harass mind and body in the way
supposed, could have occurred to Jenny
within the last month or so ; but, on the
other hand, the effects — from whatever

cause—were equally strange, and they at least were patent and undeniable.

One snow-bright afternoon in January, when Arthur and Blanche had gone out driving in the pony-carriage to fetch some novels from the railway station, Jack found himself alone with Jenny in the drawing-room.

They were seated — a very different pair—at the same chess-table at which Helen and Allardyce used to sit, and the board was before them. Jenny was a good chess-player; it was the one intellectual occupation which old Jacob pursued, and with success; and she could beat her father. Jack was but an indifferent player, and besides, he was thinking of something else.

" I can see your game, Mr. Adair," said she presently, with a quiet smile : " you mean to do this, and this."

And she shewed him how it would all have failed.

" That was my secret, I confess," said

Jack. " Will you be equally candid, Mrs. Tyndall, and tell me yours ?"

She knew well enough that he was not speaking of chess ; but she made pretence of misunderstanding him.

" *My* secret ? Nay, it is Horwitz's plan——"

" I mean the secret of your sadness, Mrs. Tyndall. You may answer, it is true, that I have no right to ask it ; nor have I any : but as the oldest friend your husband has, and because I see him changing back to the unhappy being he was at Brussels——"

" O Mr. Adair, not *that*, not *that !*" she interrupted pleadingly. She had heard from Blanche of Arthur's condition there, though not of its cause ; and the allusion was painful to her for more than one reason.

" Yes, sooner or later, he will come to *that*," persisted Adair. " Can you wonder at it, when he sees the wife he dotes upon

growing paler, thinner, sadder, daily, consumed by some direful sorrow, that she
will not speak of even to him?"

"Has he said that?" inquired Jenny
tremulously.

"Not he, Mrs. Tyndall. Is it likely?
Would he ask a question that might give
you pain, embarrassment, distress, to answer; at all events, would shew he was
conscious that his perfect trust in *you* was
not reciprocated? But if he *could* bring
himself to speak, what he would say, I am
sure, is this : ' Let me bear half this burden
of yours, true wife, and so lighten it for
both of us.' Whatever this misery may
be which has fallen upon you thus suddenly,
it is but fair, it is but dutiful, to tell him
what it is."

"Tell *him?*" answered Jenny with a
shudder. "Never!"

"Then tell *me*," said Jack.

If ever there was an honest friendly
voice in man; if ever there was a face in-

viting confidence from child or woman ; if ever there was a hand that promised help and sympathy in its tender clasp—she heard, saw, touched them then.

CHAPTER VIII.

DANETON.

"I WILL tell you, Mr. Adair," answered Jenny, "on the condition that you pass your solemn word that you do not reveal it to any human being, and least of all to Arthur. You love him better than he loves himself; you will have a sounder judgment to bring to bear upon the matter; no wicked slander against him will obtain credence with you for a moment. Yes, I will tell you."

She drew forth the hateful paper from her dress, and merely telling him where she had found it, placed it in his hand.

He read its mysterious address aloud, as a lawyer reads his brief, with care and without surprise. " That is the late Mrs. Tyndall's hand-writing," remarked he, " or else an admirable imitation of it."

These last words made Jenny's heart leap. It might, then, be a forgery, after all ; she had never thought of that. She had also never thought of something else. In her frank and impulsive acceptance of Adair's assistance, and monopolised by her apprehensions upon Arthur's account alone, she had never thought of that first paragraph of the paper referring to herself— Helen's confession of her conduct at the lasher. Had she done so, nothing would have induced her to let Adair possess himself of the fact; and her heart smote her for her forgetfulness, as though she had voluntarily committed a breach of confidence against the dead. But it was now too late ; Adair's quick eye had already perused those fatal lines. "I have read enough, dear Mrs. Tyndall," said he, smiling, "to convince myself of two things : first, that you were right not to shew this to your husband; secondly, that whatever more there is to read, it should not have disquieted you seriously for five minutes. It is sad and pitiful to think of what is here, but that is all."

"How so?" asked Jenny, trembling, yet somewhat reassured, in spite of herself, by his confident tone.

"Why, is it not plain from her first words, that this poor lady was mad when she wrote them, and, therefore, whatever follows must needs be equally unworthy of credence—cannot possibly afford ground for serious sorrow, except upon her own account?"

"There is nothing in what you have read at present, Mr. Adair," answered Jenny softly, "to prove that she was otherwise than in her right mind."

"What! Not when she says she pushed you into the river?"

" No. She did push me in, though I believe it was half by accident, and though she afterwards saved me from drowning by great exertions, and at the risk of her own life."

Jack had meant to appear quite un-moved whatever news he should become possessed of ; but his honest face shewed both astonishment and horror.

" Great heaven !" ejaculated he ; " and did you never reveal this to anybody ?"

" Never. I would never have let *you* know it, had it not been for what follows. Read on."

Jack read on, this time aloud :

" Moreover, I hereby solemnly declare that I go in fear of my life from my hus-band, Arthur Tyndall, who loves me not, but is bent on my death, in order that he may marry the girl aforesaid ; and I charge whosoever shall find this paper, to make strict inquiry into the cause of whatsoever death I shall have died : whether by sudden

seizure of disease (as it may have appeared), or by (seeming) accident, such as
the being thrown out of a carriage——"

" This is intolerable!" exclaimed Jack,
interrupting himself. " Whoever wrote
that, wrote it *after the event*—of that I am
positively certain — and is a mean and
slanderous liar!"

" I knew you would say that, dear Mr.
Adair!" cried Jenny, shedding grateful
tears. " If I had thought that, for one
single instant, you would have believed
this hateful paper, I would have died
sooner than have let you see it."

" Believe it ?" echoed Jack, disdainfully.
" If such a charge had been made, in such
a manner, against my worst enemy, against
any worthless fellow, such as Wynn
Allardyce, for instance, I would not have
believed it *then;* and to suppose that
Arthur Tyndall—— But I will not suppose it; I will not breathe his name in
connection with so foul and false a slander

—a slander, too, that bears upon its face its own refutation ; for there is malice and hate in every line. However, let us finish it :

" Such as the being thrown out of a carriage, or drowning (with both which he has menaced me), so that the guilt may be brought home where it is due."

" And so it shall !" muttered Jack ; " the guilt of this abominable device shall be brought home to him or her who planned it, or my name is not John Adair !"

" You have read the date," said Jenny timidly ; " the last day of 1860 ; that would be a few days before the late Mrs. Tyndall went abroad."

" So I see ; but it was as easy to forge a date as any other portion of this precious document."

" You think, then, that it *is* a forgery ?"

" Most certainly, I do, dear Mrs. Tyndall. The only argument against it is contained in the first portion of the document, which reveals a circumstance presumed to be known only to the supposed writer and yourself. But though you, it seems, have never revealed it to any one, the other person may have done so. It seems unlikely, it is true, but then there is no likelihood about the matter, any way. The late Mrs. Tyndall, with whom you were certainly no favourite, may have had doubts of your generosity in concealing permanently the part she played at the lasher, and she might have confided it to another, in order to anticipate your revelation of it."

Neither spoke again for some minutes; Jack's mind had suddenly reverted to Brussels, and the strange communication which Arthur had there made to him. The differences between the unhappy pair must have been great indeed, to suggest to his friend's imagination such a vision as he had described; undoubtedly, Helen had been very bitter against him; nor would it have been absolutely out of the question that she might have left this document behind her, expressly to distress him after her death, but for its direct allusion to the carriage accident, through which she had in reality met her end. That coincidence was too striking to be fortuitous, and, in Adair's opinion, stamped the document as an undoubted forgery. It *must* have been written after the event which it affected so exactly to predict. His conviction on this point became even more complete when he proceeded to question Jenny concerning the place in which the document was found. It seemed out of the question that, lying where it did, it could have escaped Mrs. Glyn's careful eyes when she put the cabinet to rights; and if so, it must have been placed there long subsequent to the late Mrs. Tyndall's death, by some unknown but hostile hand—the same, in all probability, which had forged its contents.

Of this much, Adair felt tolerably convinced; but, at his own express desire, he retained the paper, in order to examine it more carefully at his leisure.

" It is not what you thought it was, dear
Mrs. Tyndall," said he cheerfully—"an
attempt, shocking indeed to think of, on
the part of the Dead to calumniate the
Living ; but yet it is bad enough, and
reveals a fact that I should otherwise have
doubted—that you are not without a personal enemy. Can you make any guess at
who it is ?"

No ; she could not guess. She had
never made but one enemy in the world
(and that by no fault of her own), and she
was dead. Her inability to conjecture who
this foe, so bitter, so relentless, could possibly be, affected her no less than did her
previous thought, that Helen herself had
left this train of suspicion behind her, to be
ignited by haphazard. It was terrible to
think that in the neighbourhood, the village,
nay, under her own roof itself, might lurk
some malignant creature, watching the
effects of the cruel device he or she had
already put in action, and perhaps planning
others more directly aimed against her

husband's peace of mind. Suppose, for instance, such a document as she had found should meet the eyes of Arthur, jaundiced as they already were with respect to Helen, and morbidly sensitive as he was as to all that concerned his married past! How fatal might be the consequences ; and yet what prudence or foresight on her part could avert them ? Such a catastrophe might happen anywhere, it was true ; but Swansdale—the place where it had already happened to herself—seemed to be especially exposed to it. Notwithstanding her suspicions of the so-called Mrs. Montague, she could not divorce herself from the idea that this enemy was near at hand—perhaps concealing herself (for her instinct told her it was a woman, notwithstanding that Adair, in default of any other known enemy of Arthur's, had suggested Allardyce as the culprit) under the mask of friendship, and marking daily with fiendish triumph the success of her design in Jenny's sunken cheeks and hollow eyes. If she could only leave home, some portion of the oppression which weighed upon her, night and day, might, she thought, be removed from her mind ; and this object was not difficult to effect. She had only to say to Arthur : " I think change of air will do me good," and he would take her gladly, she was well aware, and whithersoever she pleased. It wounded her pride indeed—on Arthur's account, not on her own—thus to leave the home he had given her, from fear of an anonymous slanderer, whom she despised and loathed. But she felt that it was necessary to do so, for the sake of that burden, so precious to both of them, which she carried within her, and whose very life might be endangered by her terrors ; and the request was made.

Of course, Arthur at once acceded to it. It delighted him to exchange his melancholy state of solicitude upon Jenny's account for any active measure for her benefit, while the doctors assured him that her desire was of good augury, and that

she was more likely, under the circumstances, to know what would do her good
than they. As to place, since she expressed
herself as quite indifferent to it, they recommended the south-west coast, and the
London physician having a pet sea-village
of his own—that is, of his own recom-
mendation—and to whose air he had given
a high certificate—called Daneton, to Daneton they went. Thanks to its medical
patron, and to a branch line, the share-
holders of which have sacrificed themselves
to its prosperity, Daneton is now a flourish-
ing little town. But at the time of which
we write, it was but a fishing hamlet, with
not more than half-a-dozen houses adapted
for the accommodation of visitors, all of
which, however, at this season of the year,
were tenantless and to let.

There was no hotel, though a ground-
plan was marked out for one, upon a very
extensive scale ; so, of these dwellings, the
Tyndalls were compelled to take their
choice.

They were most of them very unattractive, being of the common marine lodging-house type—"scamped" as to their building, with thin walls and deceptive fronts, and very "skimpy" as to their internal fittings; but there was one residence called the "Dormers"—for what reason the oldest inhabitant of Daneton was unable to explain—which was in some respects superior to the rest, and, at all events, presented a welcome contrast to their commonplace uniformity. In the first place, it did not form any portion of a Terrace—so that what was said in its chambers was not instantly communicated to the next neighbours through the lath and plaster partition, or overheard by the stranger who might be lolling in the common balcony—but stood in its own grounds, a small wilderness of shrub and turf, surrounded by a feathery fence of tall sea-tamarisk, and a low stone wall, so near the sea, that at flood-tide and with a south-west wind the waves would break over it. It was of large size—and, indeed, at one time it had consisted of two houses with a door of communication between them—and irregular shape. The person who built it had evidently been his own architect, and despised all rules, but he had certainly not fallen into one amateur error—that of forgetting the staircases ; for of these there were no less than ten. Large as the house was, so many means of communication were far beyond its needs, and gave it the air of a labyrinth ; the rooms, though numerous, were small, and though full of nooks, and angles, and recesses, were so far like one another, that you were sometimes in doubt, after traversing two or three staircases, whether you had really arrived in another room, or had got back into one you had just left. In some of the bedchambers, the walls did not reach the ceilings, and to a nervous person there is perhaps nothing more disagreeable than the ideas of secret espionage to which *that* system of internal architecture is apt to engender.

Altogether, the Dormers—which, after
all, might have derived its name, and I
dare say did so, from the storm-windows
(as they were called at Daneton) set in its
gabled roof—was rather a weird and un-
canny sort of residence, especially when
the wind was from the sea, and cast the
sand up against the lattice-panes, as though
fleshless fingers tapped at them, and the
tall hedge of tamarisk bent low before it
with a melancholy "swish" like a ghostly
hush.   In the kitchen, which was prepos-
terously large, there were rats, it was true,
who showed their evil eyes even by daylight, and made night hideous with their
mysterious orgies; but could *all* the nightly
noises that were heard at the Dormers be
accounted for by rats ?   That was a question that many an inhabitant of Daneton
(who had never heard them) had put to his
neighbour, without receiving any satisfactory reply.   They dared not go to the
fountain-head—to Mrs. Weeks herself, who
owned the Dormers, and lived there—for

the information required, because that had
been done already by Mr. Lamb, the
house-agent of Daneton, and had resulted
in the most disastrous failure. First, she
had called him a fool ; and, secondly, she
had threatened to bring an action against
him for libel if her house should remain
unlet even for a single season. If he took
the good name of the Dormers away, said
she, mark her words, he would have to pay
for it ! And so alarmed was the meek
house-agent by this menace, that he always
made it his business to let the Dormers
first, which he generally contrived to do.
It was not difficult, indeed, to do so, since
it was the only mansion in the place, and
no great rent was set upon it. It had once
belonged to a lord of the soil—one Mr.
Waldron, to whom Mrs. Weeks had been
housekeeper ; and when he died he had left
her the Dormers—in recompense, it was
whispered, for some very confidential service performed to a female member of his
family—for her own. She was a withered

anatomy of a woman, very quiet and reserved in manner, and of a fabulous age,
but she still "got about" the "haunted
house"—as it was called by the Audacious
—with alacrity, and looked after domestic
matters as sharply as any landlady in
Daneton. She had not a bad face; but
her reticence and a certain hauteur, which
perhaps her previous connection "with the
land" caused her to maintain towards her
neighbour gossips, had earned her a bad
name. The Tyndalls, however, knew nothing of that, of course, nor of the vulgar
prejudices to the disadvantage of her residence; and as for the latter, even if they
had been aware of it, they would have held
it of no account; for, notwithstanding that
painful experience of Arthur's at Brussels,
which itself had so waned and weakened
since his second marriage that he would
now hardly have defended it against sober
argument, he was free from superstition;
while Jenny both despised and loathed it.
She was not an *esprit fort*—though her

strong sense of right, and her indepen-
dence in matters of opinion, led some of
her sex to think so—but she was singularly
unimpressionable with respect to mysteries
of all sorts. To her mind, there was quite
enough that was inexplicable in the nature
of things without drawing upon human
credulity for more wonders; and to suppose that a particular building, such as the
Dormers, should have the attribute of at-
tracting the spirits of the departed, would
have seemed not only absurd to her, but
irreverent.

Once away from Swansdale, and its
associations with the occurrence that had
so shaken her usually stedfast nerves, her
spirits began to recover their tone. The
wintry sea, the storms, the very loneliness
of their mode of life, delighted her; for
had she not always with her the best company in the world in her husband! He,
on his part, beheld with thankfulness the
colour slowly returning to his dear one's
cheek, the smile to her lips, the music to

her long silent tongue ; and though, alas !
while the shadow of her secret trouble was
undispelled, there was no fear of Jenny's
becoming " too happy" again, Arthur Tyndall and his wife could once more be termed
a happy pair.   They spent the days either
in walking on the sands, or about the
primitive little hamlet—the marine inhabitants of which were as picturesque in their
characters as were the shingle-built cottages
they dwelt in—or in taking drives in the
neighbourhood.   Nothing about it could
be described as either grand or beautiful,
but much was strange and striking.   At
the back of the village ran a river, parallel
to the sea for miles, and the tongue of land
that divided the two waters formed a
natural terrace, on which many gallant
ships had dashed themselves to pieces,
notwithstanding the warning flash of the
lighthouse at its extremity by night, and
the tall tower (raised by Danish hands)
that stood up sentinel-like by day.   From
its summit, the whole country round shewed

a level waste, marked neither with road nor hill, but bristling with ancient ruins. Here, at an elbow of the river, and there, on the margin of the sea, and there again, beside some ancient farm-house in the fields (though modern in comparison with *it*), stood tower, or castle, or abbey, all crumbling to decay. They had been doing so, however, for centuries (for their style of building was not that of the Daneton lodging-houses), and every year—not as it treats us men and women, with whom age means ugliness, and decay a loathsome change—had touched them with some new beauty, had added something to them of venerable awe. To one or other of these Arthur and Jenny made their way daily ; and in the evening, the latter would try to reproduce what she had seen in her sketch-book, while her husband read to her from some favourite volume. It was almost like having their honeymoon over again.

CHAPTER IX.

SO háppy were Arthur and Jenny in each other's society at Daneton, that they grudged even so slight an intrusion on it as another lodger under the same roof; and when Mrs. Weeks suggested the possibility of the occurrence of such an event, Arthur opposed the idea with vigour.

" I would rather pay the extra rent, Mrs. Weeks," said he, " and thereby secure his room instead of his company."

" But it is not a *he* at all, sir," remonstrated Mrs. Weeks ; " it is only an invalid lady; and she has been recommended here by Dr. Skewbald, the same gentleman as has found 'ozone,' or whatever it is, at Daneton, and is the making of the place."

"I know all that, my good woman : he recommended *us*—but not to come to the Dormers in particular."

"Yes, sir ; but this is different. Mrs. Newton, for that is her name, writes to say, or rather her maid writes for her, that a roomy house close by the sea is indispensable to her health, and that the doctor mentioned the Dormers, knowing, I suppose, that it had given yourselves satisfaction ; and as for the poor lady, sir, you will never know she has come ; for she will live in the next house, as it used to be, quite apart, and you need never so much as set eyes upon her."

Thus urged, Arthur gave a reluctant assent to the arrangement ; and in due time Mrs. Newton arrived — an elderly lady, much muffled up, and apparently without the free use of her limbs, for she

was carried out of the fly into her lodgings.
Mrs. Weeks, however, was as good as her
word, for if the Tyndalls did " set eyes"
upon the new lodger, that was as much as
they did. They saw her from the garden,
sitting with her knitting-needles at her
little window that fronted the sea ; and
they saw her twice or thrice in her wheel-
chair on the sands ; and that was all. She
kept to her old wing of the old house, and
in no respect interfered with them.

On the twelfth day of their residence at
Daneton, a telegram arrived from Adair
requesting Arthur's immediate presence in
London on important business. This
summons, so unexpected, and so vague in
terms, annoyed the husband, and alarmed
the wife. Arthur was extremely averse to
leave Jenny alone at Daneton, and yet this
reticence, so uncharacteristic of his friend,
as to the nature of the emergency, seemed
to heighten the necessity for his departure.
Jenny was once more filled with terrors in
connection with their unknown enemy.

Something must surely have again arisen from that base source to implicate her husband, and that so gravely that its nature could not be even hinted at. She besought him to let her accompany him ; but he would not hear of that—the double journey involved hundreds of miles, and she was by no means fit for such travel ; he promised to return, however, without fail on the ensuing day. Accordingly she saw him off by the morning train, and returned home dejected in spirits and full of forebodings. She had never before been separated from her husband even for a day, and in her forlorn and solitary state, the Dormers struck her, for the first time, as being a desolate and cheerless place. As she passed through the little market-place, she had noticed that the drum was up, a signal that bad weather might be expected, and the wind was blowing as if for storm. Still, anything seemed better than the gloom and solitude of the deserted house, deprived of its home spirit, and after a fruitless attempt to occupy her mind with reading, she wrapped herself up warmly and went out. For a time she walked up and down the little garden under such shelter as the low sea-wall afforded ; but—what had never happened before, and which shewed how her nerves had suffered from the event of the day— the supervision of harmless Mrs. Newton, who sat at her usual post, knitting-needle in hand, annoyed her. Whether the poor lady was really looking at her or not, could not be known, since she always had a pair of blue spectacles on her nose ; but the idea of such espionage was now become unpleasant, and indeed unbearable. That hateful Mrs. Montague, too, had been described as wearing the same appendages, and even so slight a coincidence as this was not without its effect upon poor Jenny. She left the garden, therefore, and took a long walk beside the angry sea. The whirling sand, the flying foam, were welcome to her : in the war of wind and wave, and in watching the fishing-boats, as one after another they flew for refuge into the little harbour, she forgot for a time the anxieties that consumed her. Fatigued, but yet refreshed, she came back to her mid-day meal, with unexpected appetite; which pleased her, because Arthur had charged her: "For my sake, do feed up, Jenny, while I am away." Like most husbands, he judged of his wife's well-being by the amount of fish and flesh that she consumed, which, under the present circumstances, was rather a fallacious test.

By the afternoon post came a second surprise in the shape of a letter from Blanche Tyndall, inclosing another from her husband. "What it is about," wrote she, "I have no idea; but he sealed it before intrusting it to my hands, which I consider mean."

Its contents were concerning the very thing which had been weighing on Jenny's mind all day.

" I have now found out for certain," they ran, "what, for my part, indeed, I never doubted, that the paper purporting to have been written by the late Mrs. Tyndall must needs be a forgery. The date, you will remember, was December 31, 1860. Well, while pondering over this precious production this morning, and turning it all sorts of ways, literally as well as metaphorically, I happened to hold it up against the light, when this singular fact discovered itself : *The watermark of the paper is dated* 1862. I went off at once to the makers, whose name I had also become thus possessed of, and they tell me that though it is their custom and that of the trade, to post-date their paper, it is never done to any such extent as this. The statement that has given you such annoyance must indeed have been written at least six months, and probably much more, after the death of the late Mrs. Tyndall. Thus the matter is satisfactorily settled as far as Arthur is concerned ; that is, I mean, this deliberate attempt to embitter his existence is not, what some who knew neither him nor the late

Mrs. Tyndall might have otherwise thought it, the revenge of a slighted wife, but the act of some infamous forger. Of course, it is unpleasant to feel that one has a secret foe, so audaciously malignant, but let us be content to despise, until the opportunity presents itself to punish him."

But all this well-meant consolation was thrown away upon Jenny. The discovery itself, indeed, would not have been without its interest, and perhaps its comfort, had it happened at any other time ; it was something, as Adair had said, to know for certain that that hateful document was a forgery. But of what nature could the emergency have been that had caused Adair to summon her husband so peremptorily within a few hours of sending this information to herself? It could hardly be in connection with the same subject. He would surely have mentioned something of his intention to telegraph, if, at the time of writing, the idea of such a contingency had occurred to him. Thus, so far from re-

lieving her mind, Adair's letter filled it
with alarms and misgivings, that were none
the less painful because they took no certain
shape. She would have once more gone
forth, in hopes to find some restorative for
her spirits, in the keen, fresh air again, but
the gale had now risen in great fury. The
few persons who were still about, staggered
and reeled in the fierce blasts like ships at
sea, and while she stood hesitating at the
hall door, an old market-woman, just in the
act of soliciting her custom in sea-side
fashion, was blown down, basket and all.
Jenny ran out to help her up, and bade her
sit down by the kitchen fire, and have some
refreshment; not that the woman needed
warmth or food, for she had a shop as well
as a stall in the market, and was well to do
in the world, but a craving for company had
suddenly come upon Jenny, which was altogether new to her. Her visitor seemed to
perceive this, for she observed : " I daresay
you feel lonesome enough, ma'am, to-day,
without your husband ?"

News was precious in Daneton, and everybody in it knew, by that time, that Mr. Tyndall had gone by the early train to London.

"Well," said Jenny, laughing, "that is only natural, is it not?"

"Ay, indeed, ma'am, you may say that," answered the other, sighing. "But you may thank Heaven that your goodman is not, as mine was (God rest his soul!), a sailor, and away from you at his trade on such a day as this."

"Did you lose your husband at sea?" asked Jenny tenderly.

"Yes, ma'am, I did; years and years ago, when he was no older than Mr. Tyndall, and not so gray-looking; but to this hour I never hear the wind like that but I think I hear him calling for 'Help, help, help!' It's near half a century ago, and yet sometimes the thought comes over me that he may not be dead. Not a plank of his boat ever came ashore to say so. Ah,

yes, ma'am, it's well for you as your goodman is no sailor."

"Your story is very sad," said Jenny,
pityingly; "but we have most of us our
troubles, and terrors, and uncertainties."

"Ay, ay, I daresay. Gentlefolks is no
freer from them than other people. And
alone in a house like this, they all seem to
come upon you together like, no doubt.
Do you ever hear now"—here the old
gossip sank her voice to a whisper, so that
Mrs. Weeks, moving busily in and out of
the kitchen as usual, should not overhear
her—"anything at the Dormers as you
shouldn't hear—voices and noises, and such
like ?"

"Why, yes," said Jenny, smiling.   "I
hear Mrs. Weeks speaking pretty sharply
to her maid at times (which I suppose I am
not intended to hear); and also the rats
make such a noise at night, that one would
sometimes think that a sack of potatoes had
been opened and its contents rolled down
the stairs."

"Yes, yes; but I don't mean rats : they do tell some queer stories about the Dormers, though, of course, you must know best, and they may be lies. But I have known parties to take the house for a month certain, and then to leave after the first night or two, and 'all on account of the noises.' "

" That seems to me very unreasonable," said Jenny, quietly.

"Well, well, that is as it may be ; and besides, it is not your wing of the house as, they do say, is most troubled. Now, that Mrs. Newton yonder "—and the widow motioned with her hand to the wall that stood between them and the next house— " she seems to be no more frightened than yourself ; and yet there are scores of people in Daneton as would rather sleep on the beach under an old boat than in her lodgings. It was there, as I daresay you've heard, that poor mad Miss Waldron ——Lor, Mrs. Weeks, how you *did* make me jump."

"You had better jump up and go, then, Widow Bunn," said the keen dry voice of the landlady, who had come in unobserved while the old woman was absorbed in her narrative, "and before you begin to chatter about matters which don't concern you, and of which you know nothing."

"Well, the wind do seem to have lulled a bit," rejoined the widow, as a blast, more violent than any which had preceded it, shook the house to its very foundations; "so I'll just get home while I can."

Mrs. Weeks only answered her by a scornful look, that said as plainly as any words: "You do very right not to argue with *me*;" and opened the back-door for her with her own hands.

"That's one of the rubbishy gossiping women with whom all Daneton is overrun," observed she to Jenny; "and I only hope I stopped her in time, before she did mischief. She has just been telling you, I'll go bail for it, that because I can't get rid of the rats, and the wind blows against my

windows, that the Dormers is full of un-
canny noises."

"She did say something of that kind," said
Jenny carelessly; " but I told her that my
husband and I had never been incommoded
by anything of the sort.—Who was this Miss
Waldron that she was going to speak of?"

" My master's daughter, ma'am," said
the old lady curtly. " She was out of her
mind, poor soul (though not more so, perhaps, than they as believes such tales as
Widow Bunn tells), and died here, or rather
in the next house. That makes the place
melancholy to *me*, who nursed her for many
a year, and in whose arms she passed
away; but I don't see why it should affect
others. It would be difficult to find an old
house, I reckon, in which nobody has ever
died."

" Yes, indeed," said Jenny. " I hope,
however, no foolish person will ever talk
about it to your other lodger, for, being ill
and weak, it might have an unpleasant
effect upon her."

" There is no fear of that, ma'am. The poor lady sees nobody to speak to, except her own maid ; and, indeed, she has been so ill of late as not to be able to take even her usual half hour's airing in her Bath-chair. But I am much obliged to you, ma'am, all the same : it's a great comfort to me, I do assure you, to have such a sensible lady and gentleman under my roof as you and Mr. Tyndall ; and I shall take it very kind of you, if you would say a word in its favour, when you hear it run down by them fools."

Jenny gladly promised to do this ; and yet she did not feel just then that she altogether deserved Mrs. Weeks' compliments upon her good sense and courage. When she found herself alone in her own room, with the wind howling and the sea roaring without, and within, the arm-chair vacant of its beloved occupant, the sense of loneliness and desolation recurred to her even more strongly than before. The fire was blazing cheerfully, and the small apartment was

well lighted, but nothing could dispel her
inward gloom. As the tamarisk bent and
swished before the gale, she thought of the
drowned sailor of whose fate she had just
heard, and every shriek of the wild wind
made her start in her chair, as though it
had been the maniac cry of the poor girl
who had met her end years ago, but a few
rooms off. Even the ill reputation of the
Dormers struck her with a sense of fear.
In a word, her nerves were thoroughly
shaken, and her thoughts took colour from
whatever was most sombre and morbid in
the storehouse of her mind. She sat up,
however, reading—if that could be called
such which was interrupted by a chill or
tremor at every noise without and within—
until her usual hour, and then retired to
her bedroom. A fire was burning here
also ; but the apartment looked so cold and
cheerless, that she lit not only the candles
on her dressing-table, but those on the
mantelpiece likewise, till the little room was
almost as light as by day. It was one of

the chambers, of which, as we have already
said, there were several at the Dormers,
which had once been of larger size, but was
now divided by a partition which did not
reach the ceiling.   On the other side of the
partition, but not directly opening into the
bed-chamber, was her husband's dressing-
closet ; and beyond that again was the wall
of division between the houses.   The passage outside the two rooms terminated, in
fact, in the door of communication between
them, which was always kept locked.

Under other circumstances, the knowledge that she had only to raise her voice
to make her husband hear her in the next
room, was pleasant and snug enough ; but
now, when she knew he was not there, the
blank space above the wall, with the gloomy
stretch of ceiling beyond it, was unpleasant
to behold, and only suggestive of vacancy
and absence.   Most women, perhaps, under
such circumstances, would have asked their
maid to sleep on the sofa, and keep them
company for the night, and Jenny herself

was half-disposed to do so; but she was of
a proud and independent spirit, and little
inclined to make allowance in her own case
for a weakness which she would have par-
doned, and even sympathised with in that
of another. What would Arthur say when
he came home on the morrow, and heard
that his wife, of whose good sense he had
always boasted, had been afraid to pass the
night alone! Nevertheless, she did keep
her attendant in the room rather longer
than usual, upon this or that pretence, and
before she left it, put a question as to where
the chamber bell rang, which shewed the
direction of her thoughts. " I know it can
be heard in the daytime," said she; " but
could you hear it, if it was rung at night?"

" I could not fail to hear it, ma'am, since
it rings just outside my room, where Mary
and I sleep together; for as for sleeping in
a house like this, alone, I could never do it.
It's a good big bell, and if you only jerk it
sharp enough, it would be heard all over
the house."

Here she pulled the rope to illustrate her remark, but no sound ensued.

"Well, that *is* strange, ma'am, for I hitched in the rope this very day myself, by accident, when I was doing the room, and it pealed like a church-bell." Again she pulled, and again without success.

"Well, perhaps it's the gale, ma'am, as will let nothing be heard but itself, and yet it seems to stick somehow. I'll go to the other end and see whether it does ring."

"It is no matter," said Jenny, who was beginning to feel considerably ashamed of her own pusillanimity. "The roar of such a wind as this may well drown all other sounds. You can leave me now, for I don't feel inclined for bed, and shall sit up reading for a little."

"You are *sure* you wouldn't like me to stay *with* you, ma'am?" said the good-natured maid. "It may well seem lonesome out at this end of the house, and with such a tempest out of doors——"

"No, no; thank you," interrupted Jenny

hurriedly: "I have got my books, and shall do very well." She felt quite angry with herself at having called forth such an offer by her show of nervousness. "I shall want nothing more. Good-night."

The maid left her; and she found herself listening to her footsteps along the echoing passage, and then, long afterwards, to the closing of the distant door. If she heard *that*, why had she not also heard the bell? An hour passed by. The storm seemed to have spent itself. Like a woman whose passion is almost exhausted, there were still murmurings and mutterings, and now and then a stifled sob close up against the window-pane, but there was now comparative calm. The sea still roared and rolled, but to that she had become as accustomed as is the dweller in a busy thoroughfare to the turmoil of the street. There was nothing without to draw her attention from her book, which was itself an interesting one. And yet she had only read by fits and starts : her ears were alive to the least

sound within the house. She had heard
the noise which careful Mrs. Weeks had
made in raking out the kitchen fire for the
night, and the shooting of bolts and locking
of doors that had marked her final retirement. The house was at rest so far as its
human inhabitants were concerned, and the
rats had begun their diversions. Jenny
had no " young-lady " abhorrences, and was
no more afraid of a rat than she was of a
black beetle, but still she would have
wished them quieter. What a frightful
disturbance, and how unlike any other sort
of rioting, do those animals make at dead
of night! At one time there was a charge
of cavalry through half-a-dozen rooms; at
another, a sack, not of potatoes (which was
our metaphor by daylight), but of coals,
seemed to be rolled up-stairs with infinite
difficulty, and then, at the highest step, the
sack was opened, and the contents let fall
from top to bottom. It was enough to
account for the noise in fifty haunted houses.
Hush! was that a rat in the dressing-room?

Something was stirring there, and had seemed to move a chair.

Fully aware of her increasing nervousness, Jenny was resolved not to suffer from what one well acquainted with the human mind has called the worst of nervous terrors, "a noise which the reason cannot account for:" she rose instantly, candle in hand, to investigate it, and laid her hand upon the door. As she did so, she distinctly heard what, had it been possible to be so, she would have set down to the flutter of a woman's dress in the passage without. She opened the door wide, and, holding the candle above her head, looked to right and left, but there was nothing to be seen. On the right hand lay, afar off, the room in which her maid slept, and that occupied by honest Mrs. Weeks — in a word, help and company; on the left was a dressing-room, and the party-wall that shut off the other house. She hesitated a moment as to whether she should not even now arouse her attendant, and accept the offer of her companionship for the night, but pride once more came to her assistance. She determined to explore the dressing-room. With a trembling hand she opened the door and threw it back. She scarcely needed her candle to see all within it, for the strong light from her own chamber, coming over the low partition, lit it up brightly. There was the little table with its shaving-glass, the "skimpy" chest of drawers, a heap of clothes lying folded in a chair, and a row of boots. Everything, in short, was in its usual state. What she had heard must have been fancy. Considerably reassured by the result of this examination, and congratulating herself on the effect of her own courage, she was about to return to her own room, when an impulse seized her to try the door of communication (though she well knew it was always locked) between the two houses of which the Dormers was composed. She did so, and what was her surprise and consternation to find it give to her touch—that it was open!

She closed it mechanically, and, with her fingers on the handle, reflected a moment as collectedly as she could. Who could have unlocked it, and for what purpose? Well, perhaps Mrs. Weeks herself had done so; for had she not mentioned that her invalid lodger was not so well, and might not Mrs. Newton have requested it to be left open, in case she should require assistance in the night? This was possible, of course; and even in that moment of panic Jenny accepted this sensible and matter-of-fact solution of the question; the only evidence that she gave of weakness, of her nerves being utterly shaken and unstrung—as, in fact, they were—was that, on returning to her own room, she locked the door. To attempt any longer to read her book, however, she felt would be a mockery; vague terrors were creeping over her, stealthy footfalls and trailing garments were sounding in her ear. She would get into bed and try to sleep. Before doing so, she drew aside the blind and

looked forth into the night. To her great
satisfaction the moon had risen, and showed
itself through the fleecy, flying clouds ; the
sea was a waste of foam ; the very garden
glimmered white beneath her. Even when
the candles were all put out, it would not
be dark at all. She was about to extin-
guish those upon the table, when once more
she heard that noise in the dressing-room
which had sounded so like the scrape of a
chair. She looked up mechanically to the
partition-wall, and on the top of it, with the
strong light cast full upon every feature, was
a woman's face—the face of Helen Tyndall,
who lay buried in Swansdale churchyard !
Jenny gazed at it for an instant with
staring, terror-stricken eyes, and then, with
one wild cry, that rang through the old
house from end to end, fell heavily upon
the floor.

CHAPTER X.

A HOMŒOPATHIC REMEDY.

N the same night in which that
ghastly vision manifested itself
to Mrs. Tyndall, her husband
was hurrying to Daneton by
the night-mail. The train had been late at
starting, and the engine-man was doing his
best to make up for the lost time. The
wind and the train were speeding in the
same direction, and so fiercely sped the iron
horse, that the train outstripped the wind;
yet, to Arthur's mind, impatient and dis-
turbed with the sense of peril to his
darling, it seemed to be creeping along at

the speed of a stage waggon. Though his carriage swerved and staggered in the en vious blast, he would often stand up, and, holding by the arm-straps, peer through the window, to satisfy himself of the rate of their advance, and to try to discover how far they were. It was cold, but he was in fever-heat with anxiety and object-less rage. He had been summoned to London on a fool's errand, by a telegram, of which Adair, from whom it had pur-ported to come, knew nothing ; but he would have been well content to put up with the annoyance and inconvenience to which he had been subjected, could he have felt sure that nothing worse would have come of it, not to him but to another. He could not divorce himself from the ap-prehension that something threatened his wife in his absence; that the false summons had been despatched for the purpose of separating them—of causing Jenny to be left alone and unprotected at Daneton. He had no suspicion of any particular

person ; for though he had enemies of his
own—as who has not who has mixed with
the world, and is worthy of the name of
man ?—nay, bitter enemies even, such as
Paul Jones and Allardyce—Jenny, so far
as he knew, had none. How could she
have ? Who would have the heart to
harm a being so gentle and inoffensive, and
yet so charitable towards even the arrogant
and unfriendly ? The very thought of it
made him grind his teeth and clench his
hands, so that, had he had a companion on
his journey, he might have been excused
for thinking him mad. At times he shifted
his place from side to side in the carriage,
as though it were a cage, and he a wild
beast, restless and half mad with his en-
forced confinement. At every stoppage of
the train he would impatiently thrust down
the window, and when the whistle sounded,
and the speed was slackened through tun-
nels and over bridges, he cursed the caution
that dictated the delay. On the branch
line, where the pace was slower, and the

end of the journey close at hand, his anxiety became almost insupportable, and he could hardly refrain from opening the carriage-door and leaping out, as though he would have gained time *that* way. At last, however, just as the gray dawn was breaking, they reached Daneton. There was no vehicle at that early hour, but a young sailor, whose boat he had occasionally hired, was at the station to carry his portmanteau.

"All well, I hope, at the Dormers?" said Arthur, with as careless an air as he could assume, as they stepped out together briskly towards the village.

"Why, no, sir," answered the other reluctantly; "your good lady is not well; indeed, she has been very ill; but I was to be sure to tell you, the doctor said, that she was getting on quite as well as could be expected."

"Ill?—the doctor? Good heavens! has she met with any accident?"

"Well, I don't know rightly, sir; but he has had a bit of a fright."

" A fright ! Who has frightened her ?"
asked Arthur passionately, all his suspicions, which had given place to mere alarm
at what he supposed to be an attack of indisposition, at once returning with new force.

" O, nobody, sir ; indeed, I should think
no one would be so cruel. But being alone
at the Dormers, in a gale like that of last
night, is fit to frighten any lady, in my
opinion. The wind, I've heard it said,
makes more to-do in that old house than
ever it makes at sea."

" But my wife is not one to be frightened
at the wind, lad. You are *sure* she is
getting better ?"

" Quite sure, sir ; only, the worst is—
which I didn't like to tell you—the poor
little baby-boy is dead.—Now, don't take
on, sir ; she really is getting bet——" But
Arthur was already out of hearing, having
started at full speed for home.

To think that his beloved Jenny should
have been without him in her time of
trouble, and when it had ended *thus*, that

he should not have been nigh to comfort
her, went to his very heart.   He did not
think of his own loss—much as he had
looked forward to that promise, of which
the fulfilment was not to be—but only of
his wife's pain and disappointment.   At
the house-door, Mrs. Weeks was waiting
for him, with woman's tenderness expressed
in her rugged features.

" You have heard about it all, I see, sir.
Well, your dear wife is better ; and very,
very anxious to see you.—No, not that
way, sir ; we have changed her room, so
that we might all be nearer to her, in case
you should not have returned."

At the door of a bedchamber next the
little drawing-room, stood the village doctor,
a tall, weather-beaten old fellow, with a
long skinny finger at his lips.

" Step this way, sir, for one minute,"
whispered he.   " Your wife has fallen
asleep ; and her nurse will let us know
directly she awakes.   In the meantime, I
should like a word with you."

He led the way into the drawing-room, and closed the door. Arthur followed him reluctantly enough : he longed to be with Jenny ; " and yet," thought he, with that acquiescence in the medical fiat which men of his character always pay where others are concerned, though rarely in their own case, " the doctor must know best."

" Your wife has had a bad time of it in your absence, Mr. Tyndall. Something or other, or perhaps nothing—one can never tell in these cases, without knowing something of the patient—gave her a sad shock last night. She has been prematurely confined, and the child is dead, though it was not born so ; I say that, because it may be of importance, in a legal point of view."

" But how is she *now?* How is she getting on ?" broke in Arthur impatiently.

" Charmingly—bea-u-tifully ; this sleep is itself an excellent sign ; but there is a complication. She has no fever to speak of ; and yet, she is delirious—sees things, you know. This is unusual. The question is, why does she see things?" The doctor blew out his cheeks, as though he were Rumour in some very highly coloured allegorical painting, and paused for a reply.

"Sees things! What things?" inquired Arthur in amazement.

"That is just what we want to know," said the doctor. "If it's animals, I should know how to treat her; if it's vegetables, I should know how to treat her. That is to say, if it is a wild beast, for instance, I lower the system; whereas, if it is a well-remembered landscape, I give stimulants. My own impression is, she sees wild beasts. Can you tell me?"

Arthur shook his head.

"Is she fond of exciting reading—novels with a good deal of blood-and-thunder in them, and so forth?"

"Certainly not."

"Um! Then the exciting cause is more immediate: the probability is that she was frightened by a rat. She is always looking up at the rafters of the room, as though ex-

pecting to see something unpleasant there.
I thought it better to have her removed
from the chamber where she met with this
distressing disaster ; but I examined it carefully, and my notion is, that she saw a rat—
this house is full of them—run along the
top of the partition-wall. I may be wrong,
such is my conviction. What do you
think ?"

" I remember the partition-wall," said
Arthur doubtfully, "and I've seen rats in
the house."

" Very good : then combine your information. If I am right, she must be lowered
—— That knock at the wall is from the
nurse, to say your wife is awake. I have
given orders that she is not to be left alone
an instant, night or day. Keep an eye to
that yourself, sir, for it is important. Now,
go and say a few words to her, while I step
in next door, where, curiously enough, I
have another patient, and a much worse
case, in Mrs. Newton."

Though only twenty-four hours had

elapsed since Arthur had parted from his
wife, he found her sadly altered. She
smiled upon him lovingly, but very, very
feebly ; and when he came and sat by her
bedside, she had hardly strength to take his
hand in hers. Weak as she was, the doctor
had given orders that, although she should
on no account be questioned on the matter,
yet if she seemed desirous to speak of what
had happened on the previous night, she
should be encouraged to do so. But up to
that moment she had not alluded to it. All
that was known of the affair was, that a little
before midnight a piercing scream rang
through the house, apparently proceeding
from her room, and that her maid and Mrs.
Weeks on reaching it found the door locked
on the inside. On obtaining no reply to
their request for admittance, Mrs. Weeks
had sent for a short ladder, used for getting
on the roof from the attics, by help of which
the maid had climbed over the partition-
wall from the dressing-room, and descended
into Mrs. Tyndall's chamber. She had

found her lying on the floor, close beside
the table, in a faint or fit of some kind ; and
before the doctor could be summoned, she
was taken very ill, and prematurely de-
livered of a child that only lived a few
minutes. The cause of the alarm which
had brought about these unhappy results
was totally unknown ; but the doctor—who
was a very shrewd old fellow, at least as
well versed in human nature as in the
science of his craft—judged, as we have
seen, from the direction of the patient's
eyes and the terror expressed in them, that
it was something in connection with the
partition-wall that had excited her fears.
Hence it was that, under the pretence of
greater convenience, he had had her removed into another apartment. Even to
her husband, Jenny said nothing of what
had frightened her ; but by her nestling
touch and appealing eyes, it was easy to
see what a comfort and protection his
presence afforded her ; and that even yet
she lay in dread of a repetition of that

something which, whether it was sound or
sight, had given her a shock from which
mind and body were recovering only by
very slow degrees.   All that Arthur knew
for certain was, that no rat that ever wore
tail would have so terrified his brave
sensible Jenny ; but somehow he could not
shake off the distressing impression, that
some vile person—and that the same who
had had a hand in summoning him by telegraph to town—had played a trick on her,
with results beyond what his, or her, malice
could, it was charitable to suppose, have
looked for.   With this idea fixed in his
mind, he was not only a very Argus in his
watch over Jenny, lest any further cruelty
should be attempted, but longed with eager-
ness for the discovery of some clue to this
infamous wretch who had robbed him of
offspring, and almost of wife as well ; and
it cost him no little effort to obey the
doctor's command, and avoid questioning
Jenny to this end.   At last, after many
days, and when Jenny was sufficiently re-

covered to be moved to the sofa, the doctor withdrew his veto; and taking for his opportunity a clear cheery morning, when the sea was dimpled with smiles, and the shore aglow with sunshine, and when even the Dormers itself looked bright and home-like, Arthur put the long-resolved-on question : "And when are you going to tell me, my darling, what it was that frightened you that night when I left you alone so cruelly?"

For a full minute there was no reply : then shuddering, as though the terror was on her still, and clasping his hand in woful entreaty, she answered : " Don't ask me, Arthur. Never ask me that. Believe it to be a foolish fancy not worth telling, or a something too shocking and horrible to re-late—but only spare me the recital of it. The very thought of it is painful and dis-tressing to me to the last degree."

" You have said enough, dear," said Arthur kindly, though unable to repress a little sigh. " I would not willingly give you a moment's pain."

The tears stood in Jenny's eyes. "How good and kind you are to me," said she. "I know it is not right to have a secret from you, who, I know, have none from me. I have tried to leave you one—it was very silly of me, but it seemed as though that would be some excuse for my own silence—in never asking you what took you up to town."

"Nay, darling, but I wish to tell you that whether you ask it or not; for on your knowing it may depend in some sort the elucidation of what has happened (I do not ask what it was), and indirectly the recovery of your health and spirits." She shook her head with a sad smile, but let him go on. "I mean, darling, that if there is any mystery about the matter—and there is, is there not ?—well, that, at least, ought to be explained. I was summoned to town by a forged telegram. Jack never sent it, nor knew anything about it. The only object of its being sent, so far as I can see, was to get me away from you: to leave you unprotected. In my opinion, we have been the victims of some vile plot. *I* have certainly been imposed upon ; and I think that you have also."

" No, Arthur, no." Again she shuddered, and hid her face, as though to shut some dreadful picture from her gaze, in his faithful breast.

" Well, well, I was wrong then ; and we will say no more about it."

Greatly chagrined by this failure to ex tract her story, Arthur related what had passed between them to the doctor.

" That's bad," said the old fellow thoughtfully ; "that's very bad. It's not natural, and therefore very unwholesome, that any woman should have a secret all to herself. In my opinion, Mrs. Tyndall will never be what she was again, till she has relieved her mind upon this subject. Now, look here, my good sir. I am no homœopathist— Heaven forbid !—but like cures like, as it begets it. Have *you* any little secret of your own which you have hitherto—for

reasons that have doubtless seemed sufficient for you—kept from Mrs. Tyndall ?—
You *have*, I see.   Well, if it isn't a very
damaging one—I mean not *personally*
damaging (and even if it is, that excellent
wife of yours would forgive you) ; now,
take my advice, and *tell it her*.   A sudden
confidence is what a woman can seldom
receive unmoved, and it is almost certain
to produce a reciprocity.   That might be
unpleasant in some cases—hey ?"

"No, I was not thinking of that," said
Arthur, smiling in spite of himself ; " but it
is quite true that I have a secret of my
own, never revealed except to one dear
friend."

" Female ?" said the doctor sharply,
with a twitch of his venerable eye.

" No ; male.   It is a very strange secret,
and one that I should be unwilling to tell
to any one."

" All the better : tell *her*, my good sir."

" I must add, too," returned Arthur,
" that its nature is sad—and indeed shock-

ing—and I should almost fear that the revelation of it would tend to make Mrs. Tyndall even more alarmed and nervous than she is at present."

" Not a bit of it," said the doctor confidently. " One horror drives out another, like a pellet in a pop-gun. Tell her."

Accordingly, some days afterwards, when Jenny, though still upon the sofa, was almost well enough to " get about," Arthur found occasion to administer this mental prescription. " If this bitter weather would but change," she had been saying (for the snow had been falling fast without), " and the doctor would let me leave this place, I do think I should pick up some strength and spirits."

" But the sea-air was recommended to you, my darling," reasoned Arthur, " and before you were taken ill, you seemed to be delighted with Daneton."

" Ah, yes," replied she with an involuntary sigh ; then added cheerfully : " But then we women are so changeable."

" I don't say that," said her husband gravely. " One may like a place at one time, and not at another. Did you ever notice, for instance, how the very mention of Brussels is abhorrent to me—a town which, for some days, I found by no means distasteful, but which subsequent events made so ?"

" Yes, indeed," answered Jenny, seriously enough, though not with one half the interest she would have felt in the matter had not her mind been monopolised and over-shadowed by her recent experience, from the recollection of which she could never wholly escape, " I have often remarked it, Arthur, and wondered what could have happened at a city which others deem so pleasant, to make it so far otherwise to vou."

" I will tell you, Jenny," said he gravely. " At Brussels I became the victim of one of the most distressing illusions that ever man experienced. It was within a few weeks, you know, after I had lost Helen—

What is the matter, darling ? Do I alarm you ?"

" No, no," said Jenny hurriedly. She had raised herself upon her elbow, and was looking into his face with a mixture of anxiety and awe, for which he was wholly unable to account. " Pray, pray, go on."

" Well, I am not sure that I ought to do so," said Arthur doubtfully; " for though you are the most sensible of women when you are well and strong, and would be the first to discredit such a tale under ordinary circumstances, I scarcely like to tell it you in your present enfeebled state, lest you should believe it. Still, I have long felt that I ought to have no secrets from your-self, though you keep one from me."

" Tell me, Arthur; oh, do, pray, tell me !" reiterated Jenny, unconscious, in her excitement, of this allusion to her own reticence. " It can do me no harm to *hear* of anything, believe me."

" Then she *has seen* something," thought Arthur to himself : " the doctor is right.— Well, Jenny, you must remember that, though the thing I am about to speak of did make a most extraordinary impression on me both at the time and afterwards, it was but fancy after all, as Jack, who saw me at my worst, was very resolute to urge. I was alone, and in low spirits, just as *you* were when you were taken ill the other night ; and at such times the mind is liable to false impressions, to confuse facts with fancies."

She nodded impatiently, but never taking her eyes off his ; and he went on.

" Well, to make a long story short, at a certain masquerade which I attended—not for frolic's sake, Heaven knows, but to distract my mind, which was for ever brooding upon the past—I saw the strangest vision : six weeks after she was dead and buried, Jenny——"

" I knew it ; I felt it was coming," cried

Jenny, with a face as white and damp as
the snow upon the pane.   " You saw
Helen, face to face ; *and I have seen her
too.*"

CHAPTER XI.

INEXPLICABLE.

A SILENCE followed Jenny's terrible words. She herself — clinging to her husband's arm, as though for protection against some immediate visitation of the thing she feared — seemed to have exhausted her powers of speech in that tremendous revelation ; while Arthur, even in that moment of horror, was taking counsel with himself as to whether it would be for his wife's benefit to treat what she had just related as a mere delusion, or to discuss it with her soberly, as his own inclinations urged him to do.

"You don't think I am mad, dearest, do you?" inquired Jenny timidly and in a hushed voice.

"No, dear; no. But I do think it quite possible that, at the time you saw, or thought you saw, this vision, your mind was shaken and unhinged. You were alone, you know, and perhaps alarmed by the violence of the storm; some foolish story concerning the Dormers itself might have occurred to you, suggesting ideas of the supernatural——"

"Dearest Arthur," interrupted Jenny gravely, "all this is useless. If you think it well to ignore what I, for my part, can never forget, so be it; but do not endeavour to explain it away. Not only would that be futile, but it" (here she shuddered, and once more cast around her that terror-stricken glance which always filled Arthur's heart with tenderest pity)—"it terrifies me; it seems like a sacrilegious defiance. You saw this with your own eyes, you say, or were about to say. You were so con-

vinced of the fact, that it made the very
place of its occurrence abhorrent to you,
and caused you, up to this hour, to seal
your lips concerning it, even to me. If
lapse of time and sober argument with
yourself have weakened the evidence of
your own senses, that is not my case; and
it never, never will be ! I saw your dead
wife's face, Arthur, looking into mine, not
three weeks ago; and though I should live
for a hundred years, the recollection of
what I saw will never fail, nor fade ! If
you had not told me what you have, it
would have been all the same; my conviction needed not the corroboration of your
own experience.   If you could prove to
yourself and me, to-morrow, that that had
been false or fanciful, it would count as
nothing—nothing, so far as I am concerned.
Let us, therefore, agree to be silent upon
the matter altogether, from henceforth,
until we ourselves have passed from this
world to the other; or let us discuss it
honestly, and without pretence.   The scep-

ticism which with you, if I am not mistaken, is mere bravado, assumed with the
intent of giving me courage, is to me rank
blasphemy. I have seen Helen, and I dare
not deny it."

" Let us discuss it then, darling," said
Arthur, with great tenderness, "and, as
you say, honestly ; which means, remember,
not only the acceptance of the evidence of
our own senses, but the acknowledgment
of the possibility of their having been
deceived."

A faint, sad smile of incredulity flitted
over Jenny's pale face, but she said nothing.

" In the first place," he continued, " let
me tell you what happened at the masquerade at Brussels. I was in a box, looking out on the stage, when I suddenly
found myself the object of attention of a
female wearing a black domino. She stood
alone, at but a few yards off, and seemed
to be regarding me intently. Her eyes
had an angry yet eager look in them—reproachful, and yet tender : they were

Helen's eyes.   The recognition of them as
such was complete and immediate ;   the
mere fact of their being fixed on me would
certainly not have filled me with such
astonishment and awe as at once possessed
me.   I rose from my chair ; and as I did
so, she removed her mask for an instant,
and revealed her features : they were
Helen's features !   I was as perfectly convinced that they were so as I was of my
own existence ; and · yet Helen had then
been dead and buried six weeks."

Here Arthur paused, and passed his
handkerchief over his damp brow.   The
remembrance of the scene he had described
was even now so painful and distressing,
that it brought back into his face the haggard, hopeless look that Jenny had seen in
it when, thanks to the Adairs, she met him
at the *Welcome,* and which her love and
tenderness had since so softened and effaced.
Her loyal heart, forgetful for the moment
of the terrors that consumed it, reproached
her with having compelled from his lips

a relation that had so cruelly moved him.

" And what if it *were* Helen ?" reasoned she. " What if I myself were dead, and came from the grave (as my love might well impel me to do) to look upon you."

" But you would not look reproachful, Jenny, as *she* did. It is there, alas," sighed he, " that the bitterness lies."

" But if you did not *deserve* the reproach ?" argued Jenny boldly.

" Yes, but I did," was Arthur's sorrowful reply. " I had married her when I loved another ; and she knew it. I had given her cause to know it ; or at least I had not taken sufficient pains to hide it from her. False at first, I did not maintain the pretence of affection, as it was my duty to do : I should have been patient, forgiving, penitent, tender, always."

" Poor Helen !" sobbed Jenny, with genuine compassion for her unhappy rival —" poor Helen !"

" Yes ; she deserves your pity, Jenny ;

and I do not.　I confess my falsehood and my fault; I admit—strange and unexampled as my punishment was—that I deserved it. I had no doubt that my dead wife came from the grave to reproach me for my coldness and deception.　I took the fact for granted, until an hour ago; but now I no longer believe it; I deny it.　I defy the gates of the grave to open and produce her to me!　They never did, they never can!"

"Hush, hush, Arthur!" cried Jenny in terrified tones.　"What do you mean?"

"Listen, darling, and I will tell you. Heaven is just, whatever happens, or seems to happen.　It does not punish the innocent for the guilty.　If the spirit of my unhappy wife had been permitted to haunt *me*, there was right in it; but there is something even more impossible than that the laws of nature can be suspended—namely, that He who has the rule over all things, even departed spirits, can commit a wrong. It *was* a wrong if Helen was permitted to appear to you; and therefore she did not do so. You seemed to see her, of course, as I did. What follows, then? This: that you and I have been imposed upon by the same villain. We two have some common enemy, malignant, remorseless, capable of inhuman atrocities. If ever I meet him face to face, may Heaven have mercy on his soul!"

Arthur rose from his seat, and strode up and down the room in a state of irrepressible excitement; he was furious, and yet enjoyed a secret satisfaction in the reflection that he had a foe of flesh and blood to do battle with, with whom he would one day, for a surety, settle all accounts.

As he looked at his wife's pale, woe-worn face, and thought of his dead babe, his nerves seemed turned to steel, his blood to flame; he forgot that he had never even questioned Jenny as to the details of what she had seen, so positive was he in his own mind that her senses, by cruel and wilful design, had been deceived. As for Jenny, she said nothing. Her conviction of the reality of the frightful vision that had been presented to her at the Dormers was quite unshaken ; but the last words of her husband, " We two have some common enemy," had had a significance for her which the speaker did not suspect. Now was the time, if ever, to tell Arthur of the existence of that document, which Adair had so lately demonstrated to be a malicious forgery ; but yet she hesitated to do so. The hints that he had just let fall concerning the unhappiness of his late union convinced her that these odious charges would distress him, even more than she had suspected, on account of the real basis on which they had been maliciously invented ; and above all, their disclosure would necessitate Arthur's becoming acquainted with Helen's attempt on her life at the lasher, a secret which her generous nature revolted at the idea of revealing. No ; she would not tell him, was her final decision ; she would be loyal to her rival's memory, notwithstanding that her rancour seemed to pursue her even beyond the tomb.

"You are silent, Jenny," said Arthur presently: "is it possible that you fail to understand that we have both been the victims of some infamous plot? As for your own case, can you suppose that my having been summoned to London by a forged message on the very day when this trick was played upon you—that this should have happened to you too when, for the first time since your marriage, you were left alone and unprotected—was a mere coincidence? And, if not, how is it possible that what you beheld could have been what you deem it to be? Do departed spirits send forged messages—think you— by the electric telegraph? Come, be reasonable, like your dear old self, Jenny."

These arguments of her husband, strengthened as they were by her own knowledge of the existence of the document in Adair's possession, were not without their force with Jenny. For the first time since that lonely night at the Dormers, she began to believe it possible that her senses might on that occasion have been imposed upon; but this incredulity, more welcome to her as it was than was ever faith to proselyte, eluded her embrace. Allowing for all artifices, and even for a great similarity of likeness between the face presented to her on the top of the partition and that of dead Helen—a similarity demanded by Arthur's case as well as her own—she could not yet admit to herself the possibility of her having been mistaken as to the identity. It was not the mere features, the recollection of which carried conviction with it, for the face, in fact, was altered from what it had been during life, being thinner, paler, and more aged—but the expression of the face. For the single instant (that had seemed to last a lifetime) during which it had frowned down upon her from that strange eminence, before her senses had forsaken her, she had recognised in it precisely that same look of hate and jealousy which Helen's face had worn when she had stood beside the lasher, and cried :

" Then drown, you jade !" No devilish art nor cunning, no chance remembrance of features however strong, could have reproduced *that;* and while remembering it, her heart once more began to beat with haste, her limbs to tremble, and the half-disthroned terror to reassume possession of her being.

" What I have seen, Arthur, I have seen," moaned she, in hopeless tones ; "and it was the face of your dead wife I saw, and no other."

" The face !" answered he, contemptuously. " Then did you not see the form ? Was it floating in the air like a seraph's, or looking at you like a picture from the wall ?"

" For my sake, dear Arthur, for *my* sake," pleaded Jenny, earnestly, " pray, do not jest at what has cost us both so dear."

" If I seemed to jest, Jenny," said Arthur, quickly, " it was, believe me, but in bitterness. Forgive me, darling ; and, when you have told me exactly what you saw, this matter shall be sealed between us, never to be reopened until the day when I shall lay before you the explanation of the mystery in which it is involved. That, sooner or later, I shall find that explanation, I feel convinced; and since what you are about to tell me may offer the means of doing so, I entreat you to conceal nothing from me."

With great reluctance, and with many a pause and shudder during the latter part of the narration, Jenny proceeded to obey him. She detailed every event of the day in question, from the moment of her quitting him at the railway-station to that of her retirement to her lonely room—with the sole exception of the receipt of the letter from Adair. She described even the state of her feelings, admitting that the talk of the old market-woman concerning the bad reputation of the Dormers might not have been without its effect upon her mind, and acknowledging her unusual fatigue of body and depression of spirits. She portrayed the violence of the storm, and mentioned her attendant's offer to pass the night with her as an evidence of the nervousness with which it, together with her loneliness, had affected her. She concealed nothing, in short, which seemed to make against her own view of the matter, or to strengthen Arthur's. All this, however, was but the frankness of one who has a case so strong that he can afford to concede every doubtful point to his adversary. As her story drew to its close, her every word carried with it that force which no cross-examination can shake—the force of unwilling conviction. To every question which her husband interpolated she answered briefly, and without excitement; the recollection of her own experience absorbed every other emotion. She spoke of the noises in the dressing-room, and of her visiting it; of the curious circumstance of her finding the door of communication between the houses open, and of the shock that the discovery occasioned her. But as to any thought of Helen herself having occurred to her, before, just in the act of extinguishing the candles, she had beheld that terrible apparition of her dead rival, she was positive that it had not done so. A sense of loneliness connected with Arthur himself might, and probably did, cause her to take that last fatal look up at the partition which separated the two rooms, but it was Absence, and not Death, that was in her mind. From that point nothing could shake her. "Above that partition wall, Arthur, I saw your dead wife's face looking down upon me, as surely as I now see yours; nor while I live shall I ever, alas, forget it, far less be persuaded to the contrary."

"Very good, my darling. No one shall attempt to persuade you," rejoined Arthur, cheerfully, as he stooped down to kiss her. "In a few days we shall leave this place for good and all, and in the meantime I will write to Jack, and get him and Blanche to come and stay with us, and dispel the gloom of the Dormers."

CHAPTER XII.

ACK and Blanche did not come down to Daneton, for the former had begun to have his hands too full of legal work to set his legs free, save in vacation time; idle people like the Tyndalls, they wrote, must come up to them in town, where they would be very welcome. So Arthur was deprived of the aid of his friend's sagacity in prosecuting his investigations into the subject that now so engrossed his thoughts. But, had Jack been with him, it was hard to say what could have been done more than was

done.   It is true, Arthur might have employed a detective from London, by whose
eagle eye, as he lounged before the door of
his public-house, or took his constitutional
by the beach, every soul in the place should
have been critically reviewed; but the matter was not one to be communicated even
to the most trustworthy of public officers,
and, moreover, he doubted the efficiency of
such an ally.   No clue could be obtained
in London to the person who had despatched the forged message from the telegraph office; and, quietly prosecuting his
own inquiries at Daneton, he convinced
himself that no stranger had come down
thither on the day of his own journey to
town, nor for several days before it; and,
moreover, that none such were at present
located in the village.   His investigations
were thus narrowed to the Dormers itself
and its inhabitants.   It must have been
with the connivance of some of these that
that infamous and cruel trick had been
played upon Jenny, if it had been played at

all. But which of them was it reasonable
to suspect of such a crime, and what possible reason could they have for the commission of it ?

The only tenants of the house during the
night in question were Mrs. Weeks and
her maid-of-all-work, and Jenny's maid. To
imagine that either of these should have
maliciously endeavoured to terrify poor
Mrs. Tyndall, who was a favourite with all
the little household, was preposterous, even
supposing they had the means of doing so,
which, as Arthur conjectured, must have
included some instrument analogous to a
magic-lantern. To be sure, the adjoining
house had also its occupants, a sick and
almost bedridden old woman, now said to
be dying; and her maid, a Frenchwoman,
taciturn, perhaps, in spite of herself, for she
could scarcely speak a word of English, but
who apparently had no other interest in
life beyond the care of her mistress. It
was scarcely more strange even that one
should rise from the dead, than that sober

Annette should be connected with such an outrage upon an unoffending lady. Moreover, upon cross-examining Mrs. Weeks, that honest dame most positively affirmed that the door of communication between the two houses had been locked upon the night in question, and had, according to promise, always been locked since Mrs. Newton had come to lodge with her; and that the key had never left her possession, but remained, where it was hanging at that instant, in the bunch that she always carried about with her. This was an all-important piece of evidence, and indeed, if genuine, it disposed of the whole question; for if Jenny could have been mistaken as to whether a door gave to her touch or not, her impressions might be equally fanciful respecting other matters. To that conclusion, indeed, Arthur found himself in the end, and by no means reluctantly, driven. If, generally stated, it was more likely that testimony should prove untrustworthy than that a miracle should occur, how much

more so was this the case when the testimony was that of a nervous, frightened
woman, depressed in spirits and ailing in
health ; while the miracle, on the other
hand, was as great as it could be. No ;
his poor wife's vision had been "all fancy;"
and he now regretted exceedingly that he
had revealed to her the occurrence which
had happened to himself at Brussels, the
similarity of which to her own supposed
experience had doubtless given it a greater
appearance of reality than it had worn before. The one thing that remained inexplicable, and troubled him more than he
would have liked to confess, was the forged
telegram ; but the coincidence of it with his
wife's seizure might, after all, have been
accidental, and the deception that had been
played upon him have had no other object
than to send him on a fool's errand. On the
whole, therefore, the best thing to be done
seemed to be to remove his wife from Daneton, and take advantage of the Adairs' invitation to London, where she would be free

from all unwholesome associations; and for this he only waited for the doctor to give his sanction by pronouncing Jenny fit to travel.

Exactly one month after the incident which had cost them both so dear, this sanction was obtained. The old medico had paid his last professional visit, and was giving a few parting words of advice to Arthur in the drawing-room respecting the course to be adopted for the future with Mrs. Tyndall, who was still far from convalescent, and so timid that she could not be left alone even in the daylight, when a curious circumstance occurred. There was a knock at the door, and in came Mrs. Weeks with a mysterious air.

" If you please, sir, Annette, Mrs. Newton's maid, has *come round*" (which words were italicised, as much as to say, " She is obliged to do *that*, because, as I have stated, the door of communication is always kept locked "), "and begs to say that her mistress wishes to see you immediately, if you will kindly step in."

" But I have just seen the poor lady,"
began the doctor.

" It isn't *you*, sir, but Mr. Tyndall whom
she wants."

" There must be some mistake," said
Arthur ; " unless," and he looked towards
the doctor inquiringly, " the poor woman is
out of her mind."

" She is quite herself," answered the
other ; "but, as I have warned Mrs. Weeks
here, she cannot last many days, nor, perhaps, even many hours. That is one of the
reasons, Mr. Tyndall, why I am inclined to
hurry your wife's departure from the Dormers. The decease of my poor patient
under the same roof would only add another
element of gloom to her associations with
this place."

" Without doubt, it would," said Arthur.
" But this message is quite unintelligible to
me. Are you sure, Mrs. Weeks, that you
have not misunderstood it ?"

" Well, sir, I mayn't be a good French
scholar," rejoined that lady, austerely,

"though I have heard a deal of that language talked in my time, when in service
with Mr. Waldron, whose lady was French,
and whose daughter spoke it as her mother-
tongue ; but I think I know the difference
between the doctor's name and yours, even
when spoken by a foreigner. 'My mistress
entreats the presence of Mr. Tyndall, if he
would have the goodness to *step round*,'
was what Annette said, or words to that
effect. You should see her yourself ; but
she ran back immediately, so as not to
leave her poor mistress alone."

"It is very strange," said Arthur, musing ;
"but I will go, of course, at once."

" I was sure you would, sir," said the old
lady, brightening up ; "and to save you
trouble, here is the key of the party-door,
so that you can go right through without
leaving the house."

Arthur took it mechanically, and Mrs.
Weeks left the room.

" What can be the meaning of this, doctor ?"

" Oh, it is simple enough. When folks feel themselves dying, it is generally supposed that their thoughts are monopolised with their own case; but that is not always so; on the contrary, the progress of their malady often gives them a curious interest in other sick persons. This poor lady doubtless wishes to ask after Mrs. Tyndall, who, she has heard, has been taken ill lately; and perhaps to send her some kindly message. To me, however, she has scarcely opened her lips, except to answer a question or two with respect to herself; not that many questions were necessary, poor soul; she was in a rapid decline when she came down hither, and now the end is very near indeed, as you will see for yourself."

But though to the doctor this explanation of the caprice of a dying woman seemed satisfactory enough, to Arthur it was still strange and unaccountable. He went upon his way with reluctant step, and had it not been for his feelings of humanity, would

very gladly have excused himself from such
an errand. As it was, he mused and lin-
gered, and when he arrived at the end of
the passage, put the key into the door of
communication with something more than
deliberation. A presentiment, not of evil,
indeed, but of some very unpleasant experience, was upon him, and it would have
been something like a relief to him if he
had been unable to open the door, and
been compelled to go round by the garden
way. The lock, indeed—probably through
disuse—did not turn very easily; and, on
stooping down to inspect it, he perceived a
white substance, which was also clinging to
the wards of the key. It flashed upon him in
a moment that wax had been recently used in
order to take an impression of the lock. In
that case, Mrs. Weeks' precaution to keep
the door fast had been altogether thrown
away. This discovery agitated him considerably, since it confirmed at least one of
Jenny's statements regarding the occur-
rences of that eventful night; but, at the

same time, it renewed his hesitation. At a wrench at the key and a push with his foot, the door gave way, and he found himself in the other house, which was, it seemed, an exact counterpart of its neighbour dwelling. He had entered a long passage, precisely similar to that from which he had just emerged. As he did so, the door on his left hand, answering to that of what had been his former bedroom, was opened, and Mrs. Newton's French maid appeared.

"O Heaven! how you frightened me, sir," said she, in trembling tones, and speaking in the French tongue. "I had forgotten that there was that way in, and was listening for the front-door bell."

"Some one else has not forgotten it," thought Arthur, regarding the French-woman with grave attention.

She was a stout middle-aged personage, of respectable appearance, and with so little of the foreigner about her, that but for her speech, she might easily have been taken for a fellow-country-woman of his own.

He had met her occasionally, when follow-
ing her mistress in the chair upon the sands
—when she had been strong enough to use
that exercise—and he had taken no particular notice of her. But now, as they
stood face to face, it struck him that once
upon a time, he knew not where, he had
met her, not so casually—somewhere else.
The woman, on her part too—though that
might well be attributable to their unexpected rencontre — looked confused and
embarrassed.

" Have *you* never used that door," observed he sternly, " since you have been in
this house ?"

" I, sir ? No. Why should I have done
so ? And, moreover, the landlady of Monsieur himself reserves the key." If her
surprise *was* feigned, it was well feigned :
in the expression of her profound astonishment, she even smiled.

" And your mistress — has she never
opened that door ?"

" My mistress !   What can Mon-

sieur be dreaming of ?" Her eyebrows
met the hair of her head ; her plump shoulders touched her ears. "My mistress has
not moved, since we have been at this sad
place, without my help. And now, alas !
she will never do so, even with it. Madame is dying, Monsieur." Annette heaved
a sigh that seemed to come from her very
heart, but there were no tears in her quiet
eyes.

"You are used to nurse the sick ?" observed Arthur significantly.

"Yes, indeed. I have been with Madame for years ; and she has been failing,
dying, from the first."

"But you have nursed others also; it
was your trade ?"

"Perhaps. What matters ?" answered
she hurriedly. "Hush ! that is Madame's
hand-bell ; and there are no minutes to
lose. Will you please step in ?"

Arthur would willingly have continued
to question this woman, whom he now fully
recognised as having been employed about

the convalescent wards in the hospital at
Brignon.   But her tone had a certain im-
perativeness in it, to which he felt forced
to accede;   and, moreover, she already
stood in the sick-room—-where, perhaps,.
indeed, she had taken refuge, for he had
heard no bell—to which he had been so
strangely summoned, and where, of course,
such inquiries could not be pursued.   The
chamber was precisely similar to the one
Arthur and his wife had occupied previous
to the night of her alarm, except that what
had been his dressing-room was here thrown
into it, and not divided by any partition-
wall.   The increased size of the apartment
made it look more bare and comfortless; nor
had even the same scanty pains been taken
with it to make it appear homelike and
habitable ; while the shutters were almost
closed, as though to typify the shadow that
was about to fall upon its tenant.   With
the personal appearance of the patient herself, Arthur had been tolerably familiar—
he had seen her when in her Bath-chair,

and also as she sat knitting at her window
that overlooked the garden; but as he
looked at her now, in that dim light, he
hardly recognised her, so deep had been
the ravages of disease during the last few
weeks. She was lying with her face to the
wall, which her gray hair almost touched;
and her eyes were closed. For all that she
shewed of life, she might have been already
dead.

" Madame, Monsieur is come," whispered
Annette, bending over the pillow.

The sick woman feebly opened her eyes.
" It is well," answered she in French.
" Leave us alone, Annette—quite alone.
When I want you," she added feebly, " I
will ring the hand-bell."

Annette gave a sign of assent; and passing close by Arthur, whispered: " Be
patient; be pitiful; death will be here to-
night at furthest ;" then left the room, closing the door behind her.

Her quiet tread—the footstep of one
trained to avoid stealthiness as much as

noise—passed along the uncarpeted passage, and away down-stairs.   Then all was
silent, save for the quiet beat of the wave
without, as it rose and fell on the sand.
Arthur stood in the centre of the room, in
a state of great embarrassment and discom-
fort ; it seemed to him that the whimsical
wish of the poor patient to speak with him,
if such it was, must have passed away, or
that her failing brain had forgotten his presence.   He was about to remind her of it, by
a cough, when her feeble voice once more
made itself heard : " Open the shutters."

This was not to be done on the instant,
for there were two tolerably large windows,
and the shutters moved stiffly and reluctantly on their hinges ; but Arthur, though
surprised at her request, obeyed it with all
diligence.   The full light of the noon-day
sun streamed into the room and on the bed
on which the sick woman lay.

He had got thus far, and had turned
round to address her, when he interrupted
himself with a low cry of pain and horror.

" Hush ! " whispered the patient, who had raised herself upon the pillow a little, and was confronting him with a very different face from that she had worn when he had looked upon her last. Her gray hair had been cast aside, and was replaced by light brown tresses ; her features, still pinched and worn, and with the coming change foreshadowed upon them as surely as before, were now those of a young woman. " Fear not, for I am flesh and blood, Arthur," she went on, in a tone of bitter mockery ; " though there is but little left of either."

" Helen ?" exclaimed Arthur, in horrified amazement. " You are not Helen ?"

"Yes, I am," was the grim rejoinder ; " I am Helen Tyndall, *your wife*."

CHAPTER XIII.

RECONCILIATION.

THE amazement and horror of Arthur Tyndall, on beholding this terrible spectacle, was unrelieved by one moment of incredulity. Woeworn and wan, and with the look, if not of death upon her, yet of the shadow which death casts before it, his recognition of his late wife was as complete as it was sudden. He did not doubt for a single instant that he saw before him that Helen who, in the world's belief, had been lying for the last two years beneath the mould of Swansdale churchyard. His flesh had curdled, his knees had trembled beneath him, but not with superstitious terror ; it was She, herself, and that was horror enough. But now, when he heard her mocking voice, low as a fiend's whisper, murmur in his ear, *your wife*, and marked the malice of her wasted face, another feeling took possession of him—unutterable scorn and loathing. She saw it in his shrinking form and knitted brows, and laughed a harsh low grating laugh, the very ghost of that he had once known so well, just as she was the very ghost of her former self.

"You are thinking of that woman yonder," said she, pointing with her wasted hand towards the wall that divided the two houses. "Since I am your lawful wife, you are saying to yourself : What, then, must Jenny be? Shall I tell you ?" Here a cough so violent seized the wretched woman, that to see it shake and tear her would have moved a harder heart than Arthur Tyndall's, even though it had not been evident, as it was, that a few more painful hours were all that remained to her on earth, whether for bitterness or reconciliation. He ran forward to support her, and, presently pouring out a glass of water, put it to her white lips, with an expression of tenderness and pity.

She drank ; and while he waited patiently lest she should need another draught, she clasped his hand, and, kissing it eagerly, fell back again upon the pillow in such a passion of grief as it seemed incredible her feeble frame could have endured.

Arthur's heart had already melted within him, but now he knelt down by the bedside, and mingled his rare tears with hers.

" How can you, *can* you be so good to me," she murmured, presently, " when you know what I have done to you and *her* ?"

" Hush, hush, Helen ! As for me, you have done nothing—whatever you have done—that I have not deserved ; and as for her, she will forgive you, and pray God to do so."

"No, no! No woman could do that, Arthur, on whom such disgrace and shame have fallen as I have brought on her. I am sorry for it; I repent of it; but I cannot undo it." She paused a moment to draw her laboured breath, and then went on : " I had meant to be hard and bitter to the last; but the sight of your tears, the touch of your hand, have been too much for me. O Arthur, Arthur, how I love you even yet! How could you, could you cast such love away ?"

"Dear Helen, this is no time for argument, I know," said Arthur, gravely; " but, indeed, I did not what you charge me with. I may have let it slip, but——"

"Arthur," interrupted Helen, solemnly, and looking into his tearful face, " you are speaking to one who in a few hours hence will stand before the judgment-seat of Heaven. Answer me, therefore, truly : were you not a faithless husband to me ?"

"As I hope, myself, for Heaven's mercy, I never was, Helen."

" Then I have done you wrong, indeed,"
groaned Helen ; " and her a greater wrong.
Still, you sinned in thought, Arthur ; you
wrote to her, and received letters from
her ?"

" Never, Helen, never—not one line."

" What was that packet, then — the
packet you would never show me—and
that I saw her give to you in the chalk-
pit ?   What was in it ?"

" My own letters, Helen.   Letters that
I had written to her years ago, when but a
boy, before I went abroad.   Those, and a
little trinket—which she returned to me, in
token that our love was over—that was all.
Except that once—the meeting to which
you were witness—we never met ;   we
never wrote ; we never thought of love."

There was a long silence, during which
Helen lay with wide eyes looking straight
before her, pondering many things.

" Give me the medicine, Arthur—that
one that lends me strength.   I have much
to say to you, but little breath, and scanty

time. This woman was not an angel, though you thought her so. She counted on my death to marry you."

" Indeed, she did not, Helen. In her most secret thought, I'll stake my life, she never wished for it."

" Why not ?" asked the sick woman, hoarsely—" when I wished for hers, and strove to take her life——"

" To take her life ? Dear Helen, your words are wild ; you are not yourself. Be calm."

" Arthur, is it possible that she never told you ? But no ; you must be deceiving me, for Mr. Glyddon knew it ; and, besides, I wrote it on that paper. O husband ! be true and frank with me for this one hour."

"I am speaking nought but truth, Helen. I know nothing of the matter at which you hint."

" What ! did you never hear what happened at the lasher ?"

" That you saved Jenny's life there ; yes, of course."

"And not that it was I who pushed her in ?"

"What! you? Dear Helen, you know not what you say."

"Alas! alas! I do. Ask *her*. And yet, perhaps, she may not confess it even now. Oh, do not hate me for a guilty wretch, nor curse me when I am dead indeed; but I did do it. And I have done worse, far worse, since then. Think me mad, dear husband—maddened by jealous love; not guilty; and pity and forgive me."

"I pity and forgive you with all my heart, dear Helen, whatever you have done; I know not what it is, but partly guess. Be calm, and trouble yourself no longer about the past. What is done, is done; and the best of us can but be sorry for it."

"Ay; but then some can make amends, and I, alas, can *not*. There lies the sting. Once more the medicine, and the touch of your dear hand, that seems to stir the

embers of my life. The rector says—a
good man, Arthur, if ever there was one;
who kept my secret safe ; God bless him
for it—that it is good to make confession—
the best use to which to put the failing
breath. Let me make it now, a full one;
so that, in the years to come, no more mis-
fortunes may crop up, sown by this guilty
hand, for which you are unprepared. When
you married *me*, Arthur—dear to me, when
I knew it, as when I knew it not—you
loved another." Arthur shook his head—
not very decisively, however. " You did,
you did ! I do not blame you for it ; or
rather, it was I who was to blame as well,
when, guessing at it, I still pressed my love
upon you. It was unmaidenly, as some
would say, Arthur; but it was not un-
womanly—for ah ! I loved you so. We
married ; and, suspicious of you always, my
worst fears seemed realised when we returned to Swansdale. Perhaps, if I had
spoken out, and taxed you with the wrong
I thought you did me, all might have gone

well, at least not so ill as this ; but I was
cold and cross, and you were cold, reserved,
resentful. Don't think I wish to make
excuses for myself; I know that I was
wrong, and thought unjustly of you.   There
was a man—one Allardyce—who did his
best to shame you ; a blind-worm in the
grass that would have been a viper ; he was
nought to me ; and yet, you had a juster
ground for censure against me on his account, than I against yourself on—what is
the name you call her ?—Jenny's.   That
girl I hated from the first ; and on the day
when I was witness to your meeting with
her, and saw you kiss that packet, I was a
murderer in my heart—in act almost a
murderer too.   But I repented—I thank
Heaven for it—and strove to undo what I
did in haste, as she will witness.   Then,
because she kept my secret, and was
generous to me, and because you thanked
me for having saved her life, my hate re-
doubled.   At one time in my bitter, love-
less life, I had longed to die ; but now,

being ill, and feeling that the seeds of death were in me, I desired to live : "For if I die," thought I, "Arthur will marry her." Then we went abroad—to Brignon. You recollect the misery of that time. I will not dwell upon it. Well, even then, it entered into my heart that I would leave you, and hiding away somewhere, die, so that you should never know I was dead, or be able to take this woman for your wife ; and with that intent I put money by me, which was afterwards used for a still worse purpose. When the accident happened, I was taken to the hospital, like yourself. I mended and grew better, but was still far from convalescent, when some catastrophe in the town—the falling of a circus-tent— made urgent demand upon the hospital resources, and I was removed into the convalescent ward, to make room for some young girl who died that very night. In the unwonted hurry and confusion, *the name upon the bed-head was not changed*, and when (as I afterwards heard) my maid came

as usual the next morning, and, as I believe,
Blanche as well, to see me, they were
told that I was dead.   They went up, and
saw the corpse stretched out in my old
place, with the sheet over it, and did not
dare, I suppose, to lift it.   A suspicion of
what had occurred came over me when I
found that no one visited me as before ;
and in a few days, keeping very quiet, but
listening for all that was said around me, I
heard the tidings of my own death, and of
how my body had been carried away by
the rich English milord and ladies to be
buried at home.   I heard also, with a joy
more shameful than grief would have been,
that you were getting well, for the vile
design over which I had long been brooding had already taken hateful shape.   The
germ of it was due to a slight thing enough,
yet one which by its association might well
have touched my heart, had it not been
changed to stone by jealousy.   On that
river-voyage that we two took together, in
what seems such a far-back time "—for the

first time, Helen's voice, which, though feeble, had been hitherto firm and resolute, here began to tremble—" in that bright day, when earth, and sky, and water seemed to rejoice with me because of your dear love, then were some stories told; one by the man Allardyce, of some one who had married in England and been divorced in Scotland, and who, marrying again, had been claimed by his first wife as her rightful husband, to the confusion of the second; and again, some tale of Blanche's about the chalk-pit above Swansdale being haunted. You will remember *that*, because you met this girl—to whom you had plighted troth and broken it—just after the tale was told, at Swansdale Lock."

Arthur bowed his head so low and sadly, that it seemed less in assent than in contrition.

" Well, out of those two tales I shaped my plan. That you would marry this woman — as you did — I felt convinced; and my intention was to keep out of your sight and knowledge till you should do so, then break in on your guilty happiness, and change it to misery and shame. I meant to haunt your home, like the ghost that Blanche had spoken of, [and terrify this hateful woman, if not yourself. All this I thought of—gloated over—as I lay in bed, supposed to be unconscious, until one day came in a woman who had been employed elsewhere in the accident wards, and recognised me."

" That was Annette ?" said Arthur.

" Yes; Annette. She is a faithful, innocent creature, and has been very good to me. At first, I tried to bribe her to silence; but that failing, I told her all, and more than all my wrongs—how that you had ill-treated, beaten me, and even designedly caused the accident by which I had so nearly lost my life ; and she believed me. I persuaded her that my only chance of happiness for the rest of my short life—for though I had recovered from the direct effects of the fall from the carriage, it had

injured what were already diseased, my
lungs, and I was doomed to die—was to
keep out of your way, and give no sign of
my existence. In this she consented, out
of pity, to assist me; and to make sure of
her silence, when I left the hospital, which
I did under a false name, I took her with
me. I had sufficient money to support us
both, laid by, as I have said, and hidden in
notes about me; and I followed you—not
telling Annette that I was doing so—to
Brussels. Why so? you will say. I
cannot tell you why. My love for you was
dead, and yet I longed to look upon your
face once more. I watched and dogged
you. Your pale looks smote my heart;
above all, it melted towards you because
you showed no sign of returning to England
where that woman was. One night, however, I saw you start from your hotel in
company with some friends for the masquerade : that made me bitter again. To think
that within three weeks of your Helen's
death, you should drive away all thought—

remorseful thought, as I imagined it to be, remember——"

" It *was* remorseful," murmured Arthur.

"Well, to think that you should seek enjoyment in such a place, and find it so very, very soon, was wormwood to me ; and, instigated by headlong passion and jealousy of I know not what, I followed you."

" I saw you in the theatre," cried Arthur. " I knew that it was you even before you removed your domino, and froze me with your ghastly, scornful look."

" I know it," said Helen. " It was the madness of the moment ; I perilled all my plan when I did that, I know, and yet I could not resist the temptation to reveal myself. 'He will not believe even his own eyes,' said I to myself ; and yet, in my secret heart, I thought you would. Notwithstanding my unforgiving wrath and malice against you, and the danger to which I knew I had thus exposed the execution of my cherished vengeance, it was a satisfaction to me that you recognised your

Helen—that rather than deny the face you had so often kissed, you accepted the miracle. I watched, and saw that it made you a changed man. A hundred times I had made up my mind to write to you, and confess all, and then to come and meekly beg forgiveness of you ; but I did not. I said : ' I will wait a year and a day,' when, as I had heard, widowers are free to marry. Then suddenly, on receipt of some message by the telegraph, you left Brussels— for Swansdale, as my heart foreshadowed, and I followed you. While lurking in the neighbourhood disguised—I was at the inn at Medhurst within four miles of you—I learned the worst I feared had come to pass—that you were engaged to my rival. Then began my madness ; my love for you died out, or seemed to do so, to its last spark, and my one desire was for revenge. I followed you to London. There, although I thought my heart was already brimmed with hate against the woman that was to succeed me, it found room for more ; for, by one I set to watch your movements and all you did, I learned that my mother—my own mother—had received her; that she regarded with patience, if not with favour, the girl that was to usurp her daughter's place! O Arthur! if it seems hard to die and be forgotten, how much harder to live on, and watch your memory fail and fade away, and mark the image of yourself, that you had deemed imprinted on a loved one's heart for ever, wax dim and wane! A dead man out of mind, is dead; and (unless he has earned hell's torments) knows not how soon those near and dear to him throw off the heart's allegiance or — worse, a thousand times — transfer it to another; how smoothly runs that round of life without him, of which he was once the pivot! But I—false to the core—was, for my falsehood, doomed to be the spectator of my own oblivion! O Arthur! I have indeed been punished for my sin; and when I wronged you most, deserved your pity. Pity me, for pity is akin to love, they say;

Rcconciliation.

or, if you cannot pity, think me mad—for
mad I was—mad from the first, to think of
such a fiendish, foolish scheme ; and mad-
der made by the sight of that which, from
the first, I knew that I should see—this
woman taken to your heart, your arms !
Ah, how I hated her, and cursed you both !
I could not make you criminal—a felon—
by intermarrying with her while I was
alive : that was done in innocence ; but
what I could do, that I did, and gloried in
it. This girl, who thought to be your wife,
was but your paramour ! Oh, that thought
was sweet ; and if she should have offspring—the children that you longed for,
and that Heaven had denied to me—they
would be bastards ! Ah, that was balm !"

The colour came into the dying woman's
cheeks, and in her eyes a fire of triumph,
and her voice rang for the moment like a
trumpet. Then she fell back and gasped,
what seemed her last ; and once more
Arthur put the medicine to her lips, and

once more life flowed back a little, and she went on in a hoarse whisper :

" You married, and went abroad. I heard of you in France, in Italy, so happy, so unlike the man you had been when wedded to your late unsympathising, unessential spouse. They spared me nothing —why should they ?—those whom I employed to tell me all—in their reports of you. You were coming back, like two young lovers still, to Swansdale. I went down before you, and in tourist-guise gained access to the Hall, and left a paper, where I knew your wife would find it, dated two years ago, and setting forth how that you wished me dead, that you might marry her, and had sworn to kill me ; and that if I did die on a sudden, it would be by poison ; or by any seeming accident, such as the being thrown out of a carriage, it would be no accident, but by your malice and intent.—You turn your face away ; you loathe me : well you may. But I have not done yet ; hear all—hear all ! This set your wife a-thinking—as I knew it would—upon our miserable life together: and Was it possible that you had thus ill-used your Helen? And she fell ill, and lost her spirits—though not her looks; she would not, curse her! lose her fair, soft looks, that had entrapped you so—with keeping the secret from you. This went on for months, and you were wretched, both. I felt no pity, not a grain, for she was quick with child; and I, the barren wife, loathed her for that more than for all. For her health's sake, you came to Daneton. *I* needed Daneton air too. The doctor said that I might prolong my life to half a year, perhaps (but he was sanguine there), by going thither. And with that excuse, I ventured to house myself beneath the very roof that sheltered her and you. There was no time to spare, if I would see the harvest of that vengeance of which I had already sown the seed, ripen, and cut and gathered in. Up to that moment, I had felt no penitence nor pang of remorse; no-

halt of purpose.   Finding you happy here,
I looked to find it strengthened, and myself more resolute for evil ; but it was not
so.   At times even, as I watched you both
—you little knew whose eyes were on you,
Arthur—in the garden and on the beach,
so satisfied with each other's company, so
well pleased with all you saw, and all you
did, together—at times, I say, the thought
would cross me : ' Are they so very guilty,
after all ?   If they did wrong me while I
was alive, could they be so light of heart
and so content ?'   I had told Annette I
did but come hither to feast my eyes in
secret upon the man I had once so dearly
loved before I died ; and there were
moments, nurse my passion against you as
I would, when my heart did yearn towards
you, as it does now, husband—and I re-
lented from my purpose.   But they were
few—few as the lucid intervals that light
the gloom of madness.   I had sworn to
take full vengeance, and I kept my oath.
I could not hope to see this bastard born,

and gloat my eyes on the disgrace brought
forth with it upon its mother : my time was
too short for that ; and if from any cause
you should have gone home, or elsewhere,
I was too ill to follow you. But I might
appear to her as risen from the tomb, in
some lone night ; and though I died the
next day, the remembrance of that ghastly
vision should haunt her, as it had haunted
you—but worse—until her latest day. If
she had not told you of that paper—and I
did not think she had—she would be sure
to take it as a confirmation of the cruel
charge I had made in it against yourself :
my unquiet spirit, she would think, was
crying out for vengeance, retribution.—O
yes ; I know it was a demon's act ; and
when you look upon me thus, Arthur, I
feel as though I were in the place of
demons ! Yet think, O think, that ere
yonder sun has set, we two shall part for
ever ; and strive in this last hour to
pity and forgive a woman wronged !"

He did not speak, but still kneeling by

the bed, kissed the wasted hand that clung
to his own, as though in fear lest he should
rise in wrath and leave her.

"It was a hateful act, dear Arthur—
a vile and wicked deed, and false and
fraudulent from first to last. I took an
impress of the lock of the door of communication between the houses, and had a
key made from it in town ; and when all
was ready, I caused the message to be sent
that took you thither, and left her here,
defenceless and alone. She has told you
all that happened, doubtless ; but she does
not know that that which killed her child
has saved her honour. If it had lived,
remember, it would have been the child of
shame. In that, my vengeance over-
reached itself. Moreover, what half slew
her, has made an end of me : the dragging
myself by night from this sick-bed, and
climbing on the chair to shew myself above
the wall to her, well, all that has quickened
what before was fast approaching ; and at
last I die, and leave her free."

" And you repent, dear Helen ?" whispered Arthur eagerly. " You are sorry that you injured one who never meant you ill ?"

" Yes, yes ; I do—I am. When she becomes your wife—for *I*, I alone am your wife, Arthur, while I live—tell her, tell her that I was sorry. And, Arthur—lean down, lean down, and listen ; I have but a minute more : don't tell my mother ; don't let her ever know ; dear soul, kind soul. And—and—when you think of *me*—remember, you did love this woman, all along, better —better far than me—and pity, pity your poor wife—your *wife*, who lacked your love !"

There was no sound more but the lap of the wave without ; she was dead, with her hand still clasped in his, and her last look fixed on his face. Pity her! He had never loved her so dearly, or so deeply, as at that moment. When he had thought her dead before, he had been sorry, remorseful, wretched, but he had never shed the tears that he shed now.   If she could have waked to feel them falling over her cold cheek, she would have said : " I must be dead indeed ; and this is Heaven."

CHAPTER XIV.

GRISELDA.

RELIEVED by this passionate out-
burst of grief, the traces of which
he made no effort to conceal,
Arthur summoned Annette.

"It is over, then," said she simply, perceiving what had happened at a glance, and
reverently kissing the forehead of her dead
mistress. "That is well. Heaven has
taken her into its hand out of yours, sir;
and let us hope," she added reproachfully,
"that she will find better treatment there."

Arthur gazed at the woman without
hearing what she said, and almost, indeed,

17—2

without seeing her. Her manner softened at seeing him thus, and touching his hand, to call his attention to her words, she continued: " Knowing that this must happen either one day or the next, Mr. Tyndall, I have locked up such valuables as Madame possessed, with her little store of money ; and here are the keys. She is no longer in my charge, but in that of her husband."

" Hush, hush," returned Arthur, laying his finger on his lip. " If you loved your mistress, you will obey her last words, which expressed her wish for secrecy. Your looks imply that I have not done my duty to her hitherto, and you are right ; I have done far otherwise : still if she could speak, she would tell you that I have not been what you think I am. I say this much, not in my own behalf, but that you may know she has one genuine mourner besides yourself. As for you, I know that I leave her—as for the present I am compelled to do—in loving, reverent hands. With respect to the money and the jewels, so far as I have power to give them—and I suppose I have—they are yours. Moreover, I shall take care that henceforth, throughout your life, you want for nothing."

"Monsieur is very good and kind to *me*," answered the woman, significantly, and looking tenderly at her dead mistress; "but ——"

"But you cannot take a bribe to wrong the dead," interrupted Arthur. "What I offer is no bribe, however. If you went out into the village street, and cried aloud the truth: ' Here lies this fellow's wife,' that would make no difference. I only give you what your fidelity has earned. But I tell you again, in this dread presence, before which I should not dare to lie, it was her latest wish, for her mother's sake—I do not say for mine—to keep this matter secret. She *was* my wife; I was her husband. But to say so now, would be to disobey the dead, and wrong not me, but the innocent. That is the truth, so help me Heaven!"

"I believe you, sir," answered the woman, after a moment's pause; "and I will keep your secret safe. There is a fear, however, that Monsieur's own looks may reveal it. If I saw you in the street now, I should say: 'There goes some new-made widower.' Kiss her once more; then wash your eyes and go."

It was curious to see this quiet woman thus dictating to him, as though he were a patient in her charge, and him obeying her meekly; but it was well for Arthur that such a helper was at hand, well used to deal with Death and Mourners, and to whom all tattling was by nature distasteful; since, had it not been so, the gossips of Daneton would have found some means to understand her alien speech, had it been Norwegian.

Leaving the house that held his beloved dead by the outer door, so as to avoid his own, Arthur went to the railway station, and despatched a telegram to Adair, then hastened back to Jenny.

" Do you think you could bear a journey to town," said he, " this very day ?"

" Indeed, indeed, I could," answered she joyfully. " Don't look so grave ; it will not hurt me, Arthur ; it will do me good. But why have you resolved on it so suddenly ?"

" The doctor would not give his permission before, you know."

" And what a time you have taken at last to get it, dear ! Why, he has been with you for hours, has he not ?"

" Yes ; we had a long talk together ; but it is settled now ; and if you really do feel strong enough ——"

" My darling, I feel almost well already." Her heightened colour, and the ardour of her eyes, spoke her delight at the prospect of leaving the Dormers, though, hitherto, she had done her best to conceal her impatience to do so.

" Yes, but you are not well, dear Jenny, nor nearly well. Though out of the doctor's hands, he leaves his deputy ; your nurse is to accompany you." Her countenance fell

at this; she was no malingerer of fashion
—not a woman who likes to be coddled and
made much of on the score of illness, when
there is naught the matter.

" But that is surely unnecessary, Arthur."

" Believe me, it is *not*, dear," said he
gravely; " and when we are once off, Jenny,
I will tell you why."

That was enough for her, and more than
enough, even had she never learned his
reason; but in the meantime she did learn
it, or thought she had done so.

No sooner were they in the railway carriage, and alone, than she said tenderly:
" I know why we take this sudden journey,
Arthur, and why we have brought nurse
with us, and why you look so grave and
sad, my darling."

" Do you ?" replied Arthur, quietly.
" Why is it, Jenny ?"

" It is because of poor Mrs. Newton's
death."

" It is, my dear."

" I knew it. When Mrs. Weeks told

me what had happened, I said to myself at
once: 'Dear thoughtful Arthur deemed
that this sad occurrence taking place under
the same roof would render me depressed
and nervous.' But it has not done so, indeed, my darling. I wish I could have
been of any use to the poor lady. It was
very sudden, surely, though not, they tell
me, unexpected. And how came she to
send for *you* ?"

"Well, as the doctor rightly suggested,
chiefly upon your account. When folks are
dying, they take an unwonted interest in
others who are sick and suffering. It was
a sad scene, of which we will not speak just
now. But you were wrong about the nurse.
I brought her, Jenny, because it will be
necessary, when we reach town, that I shall
leave you."

"*Leave* me ? O Arthur, why ?" Then
added hastily: "But I am sure there is
some good reason—a painful one, by your
sad face ; and I will not pain you by asking
for it. But oh, dear husband, it is not for

long, I trust ! Without *you* ——" She
shuddered ; the recollection of what had
happened when he had left her last flashed
on her mind, though she would not distress
him by referring to it—" without *you*, the
days will be very long.   Will you be absent
many days ?"

He shook his head ; he could not trust
himself to answer, when he thought of what
was taking him away from her.

" Are you sure, Arthur, *quite* sure, that
it would not do you good to tell me ?   If I
could, by sharing it, bear up for you even
but a little portion of the burden which I
see is pressing upon you, it would be such
a comfort to me, such a happiness !"

" No, Jenny, no," answered he hoarsely ;
" that cannot be.   You can help me only
by leaving me to myself, by not questioning me, by placing all the confidence in me
of which your loving nature is capable, until
the time comes—as it will come some day
—when I can tell you all.   Will you promise me to do this ?"

"Indeed, indeed, I will, Arthur."

That she would do so, he felt very sure. She had always striven to anticipate his wishes, and now that he had expressed them, was it likely that she should fail in her obedience ? But his heart was full of trouble and perplexity. To confess all to her some day, as he had just said, would be positively necessary ; but how should he make amends for the wrong that had been done her, without the knowledge of others ? Without taking at least one other person, such as Adair, into his confidence, this would be full of difficulties. To ponder upon these, and to plan how to overcome them, though a distasteful task enough, was better than to let his mind revert whither it ever strove to wander—to Helen. In either case, however, it was a melancholy time enough with him ; and the efforts which poor Jenny made to console him, by a show of increased affection and devotion, only rendered him more wretched. He seemed to himself to be obtaining them

under false pretences.   At last, perceiving
that her loving ways had lost their power,
and yet, that, when left to himself, he grew
more wretched, she began to talk of ordinary matters, such as how long would their
journey last, and where did he propose to
stay in London.

"I have telegraphed to Jack," said he.
"We are going to the Adairs."

"But, remember what a little house they
have, dear.   They offered to take us in, it is
true—though you remember what Blanche
said about their scanty room—but I am
almost certain they will not be able to take
in nurse."

"They will take in you and nurse—not
me, dear," returned Arthur,   "The business at which I hinted will take me from
you at once—to-night.   I shall leave you
in Blanche's hands, however, knowing that
you will be as well cared for there as in my
own.   In a week or less I shall come back
to you."

Despite all her firmness and good sense,

this unlooked-for tidings of her husband's immediate departure from her struck cold to Jenny's heart. She was not, perhaps, so fully recovered from her illness as she endeavoured to persuade herself : at all events, she made no answer, for she could not, but turned her head away to hide her quiet tears.

It was a long, sad journey for them both. Arrived in London, they drove straight to the Adairs, who received them with affectionate welcome. In an hour afterwards, almost all of which time he had spent in private talk with Jack, Arthur left the house, to go, Jenny knew not whither, and had forborne to ask. That one at least of her entertainers knew, she felt convinced ; which made her trial the harder. But yet, Griselda-like, she was patient, and put trust in him who seemed to have no trust in her. Day after day passed by without a line from him, but on the sixth day, in the morning, he returned. Not a word of complaint, nor of remonstrance, even then did Jenny breathe, but took her husband to her arms with a thankful heart. There had been a something in the behaviour of her host and hostess towards her, in his absence, so commiserating, so compassionately kind, that it had filled her with the dread foreboding that he was gone for ever.

" And you do not ask me where I have been, Jenny ; or why I was so cruel as not to write !" cried he, admiringly.

" Nay, my darling : when the surgeon cuts and probes," was her reply, "the patient does not ask, ' Why does he torture me ?' I knew that you would not thus wring my heart, if you could help it."

" That's truth, my love, my own, Heaven knows !" he answered. " The trial, however, of your patience is not over yet."

"Are you going *again* to leave me, Arthur ?" she put in, piteously.

" No, darling ; never, never ! But you must still trust in me implicitly, and without questioning, for a few hours longer, whatever happens. Will you ?"

"For a few hours!" she answered, lovingly. "For life, if need be, husband!"

Then Blanche came in, with her bonnet on, and said : "It is time, Arthur;" and looked towards Jenny.

"Blanche and I are going somewhere," said Arthur, tenderly ; "and you must come with us."

A carriage was in waiting at the door, and took them off, all three. None of them spoke throughout the drive, which was a very short one, and ended at a church porch.

"We get out here, darling," whispered Arthur. "Remember your promise, and have faith in me."

Jack Adair was waiting for them on the steps ; but the church was empty, save for the clerk, who closed the door behind them. From the vestry, however, came out a clergyman in his robes, and took his place within the altar-rails.

"What is this ? What are we going to do ?" whispered Jenny, in wonder.

"We are going to be married, my darling. There was a flaw in the first."

Jenny trembled excessively; her heart beat violently; her face was suffused with blushes—not a bride's; her senses reeled: but she called to mind her promise, and summoned all her courage; and by the time the priest began to read, was calm. The kindly pressure of honest Jack's hand, as it gave her away, went far to reassure her. Only once she forgot herself; and when the time came for inscribing her name in the register, would have written "Tyndall," but for Arthur's watchful interposition. "That is often done," observed the clergyman, good naturedly, and little thinking why it *was* done. Then Blanche embraced her tenderly, and, taking Jack away with her, left Arthur and herself to go home alone.

CHAPTER XV.

HEARTH AND HOME.

THE revelation that Arthur had to make to Jenny was necessarily a long one, and affected her by turns with pain, and shame, and pity. The only consolation was, that the mystery of that ghastly spectacle which had so shattered her health and weighed upon her spirits, was by it resolved. He told her all he knew, and also how that he had left her to return to Daneton, and followed the remains of Helen to the grave. " I could not write to you the truth, my darling, could I ? So I did not write at all."

Arthur had thought of taking Jenny
abroad with him immediately after their
second marriage, but he did well in suffering himself to be persuaded by the Adairs
to remain for a few weeks beneath their
roof : a woman's love and sympathy was
what his wife now needed even more than
his own passionate affection, and in Blanche
she found it.   Not a word ever passed the
lips of either in blame of Helen ; but of
the two, Jenny's thoughts of her were the
more charitable and forgiving.   The revenge that she had taken upon her had
indeed been great and terrible ; but had she
not (as she reflected) been robbed by her of
Arthur's love ?   There was an excuse for
her in that to Jenny, which there was not
to Blanche.   It was years before the latter
could come down to Swansdale and hear
unmoved the thunder of the lasher, where
Helen's crime had been so nearly consum-
mated ; and could look upon that grave in
the churchyard, where Helen did not lie,
without a shiver.   But in due time, for

Jenny, Swansdale had associations of another kind, so bright and glad, that it dispelled all surrounding gloom. She had children—boys and girls—who made the old house loud with mirth, and a playground of the ancient garden. Hand in hand, these would visit the cottage, and speculate, not without some childish trepidation, upon what manner of man that Uncle Magus had been, of whom they had heard so much, yet understood so little; or question old Giles secretly upon that mysterious and absorbing topic, the first Mrs. Arthur Tyndall. That she could not have been so good or beautiful as their own mamma, was certain; but they like to hear him tell how fair she was, and how Uncle Magus had loved her. Grandpapa Renn was a living enigma to them, but they enjoyed nothing better than an afternoon visit to him (with its terrible passage over the lock bridge, where the girl clung tightly to her mother's hand, and the boy sent a thrill to her loving heart by his temerity),

when the old man would sit out on the
lawn, and give them pipes to blow bubbles
with, and converse about what they deemed
to be another inexplicable member of the
family—the Mother of Sherry. When he
told his pretty grand-daughter (who was
his favourite of the two) that she would
never be one-half so beautiful as her
mamma had been, the child assented to
that statement ; but when he added that
she might have had a lord for her father,
and asked how she would have liked *that*,
she answered, after much reflection, that
she preferred matters as they were, and
" her own papa" to any lord. The Herb
Valerian does not, therefore, it would seem,
affect the female mind till after four, which
was little Jenny's age at that time.

To these inquisitive young people, Mrs.
Somers, who occasionally visited the Hall,
and never without bringing a cargo of
sweetmeats for them, was another family
riddle. In a moment of Dutch courage,
produced by eating too many French sugar-

plums with liqueurs inside them, Master
Arthur had once called her "grandmamma,"
which title the kind old lady had accepted
very readily ; but when he added : " Then,
if you are grandmamma, you must be wife
to grandpapa at the lock," she by no means
took it in such good part, but cuffed his
ears, and shut up the bonbon box for the
afternoon. It was the only occasion on
which that excellent lady was ever known
to have been " put out." Even when the
observant child once asked her : " Why do
you call me Harthur, Grandmamma Somers,
when my name is Arthur ?" she answered
him, with her usual good-nature, that it
was by reason of a " 'uskiness " in her
throat. This explanation of her infirmity
had been so often given, that there is no
doubt she believed it to be the true one ;
and she clung to it to the last. But we
don't get to Heaven the less, it is to be
hoped, through pronouncing it without the
aspirate ; and when she died — which
happened in London, with her favourite

Arthur Tyndall and Blanche Adair about her pillow—the world might better have lost many much finer ladies and much better grammarians than honest Mrs. Somers.

So tender was the good old lady's heart, that it pitied those it ought to have despised. A little before her last illness, she had quite a battle-royal with Jack Adair in behalf of one she had little cause (had she known all) to defend — Mr. Wynn Allardyce. There were rumours that, after having been a defaulter at Tattersall's, that gentleman had taken to several bad courses, but especially to drink; and one day Adair brought word to Swansdale of his final degradation.

"Who should I see dragged out of the train at the junction this morning," observed he at dinner, "for cardsharping, but the Honourable Wynn Allardyce!"

"Oh, impossible!" exclaimed Mrs. Somers pitifully.

"But, my dear madam, I saw him with my own eyes. He had a bonnet too——"

"Then, depend upon it, he only did it for a joke, poor fellow."

"I mean a confederate, madam," explained Jack; "who was taken up in his company, and in whom I also recognised an old acquaintance. But our honourable friend — poor 'Lardy'—looked much the greater scamp of the two."

"Well, for my part," said Mrs. Somers, "I cannot imagine that Mr. Allardyce could ever look anything else than quite the— what do you call it ?—the haristocrat."

"My dear madam," answered Jack with some little impatience, for he knew the utter worthlessness of the man well, "I don't doubt his aristocracy; but he was a rogue in grain, a scoundrel from skin to skin."

"Well, well," urged the kind old lady, "remember he was a young gentleman of title, and had naturally been spoilt from his cradle, and flattered, poor fellow, by everybody that came in his way. It is no wonder if such high folks, when they come down a peg, and want money or anything else, think they have a right to obtain it in any way."

"That is an excellent argument against the existence of a hereditary aristocracy," answered Jack, laughing ; "and I'm sure I've no fault to find with it on that score ; but——"

"Jack, for shame!" ejaculated his wife.

"Mr. Adair, I'm astonished at you!" exclaimed Mrs. Ralph Tyndall, who, with all her respect for her son-in-law, never called him by his Christian name ; it was not her way. Upon the whole, it was evident that Jack was in a minority upon the question of the Honourable Wynn Allardyce's peccadilloes. With all his faults, those three excellent ladies could not forget that the culprit was a sprig of the Herb Valerian.

"Well, well," said Jack, who was much too sensible to argue with his fair antagonists on such a subject ; "but you have not

asked me who his confederate was. It was
no other than his old friend and ally, Mr.
Paul Jones—his 'pretty Poll,' as he used
to call him, and in a very moulting state, I
do assure you."

" I never liked Mr. Paul Jones," observed
Mrs. Ralph Tyndall quietly.

" Liked him, mamma!" exclaimed
Blanche; " I should think not, indeed.
He was the most odious little creature!"

" His appearance was certainly unfortu-
nate; but he did his best to make himself
agreeable, poor little fellow!" said charitable
Mrs. Somers. That good lady had not
"an aversion" in the world, nor had she
ever made an enemy in it. " Happy is the
woman who has no biography," was a
proverb that found its example in her
smoothly flowing life. She never knew of
her daughter's second Death; nor did any
one know, save those five persons to whom
it had been necessary to disclose it. No
one else suspects, who reads in Swansdale
churchyard the inscription to " Helen, wife

of Arthur Tyndall," that beneath it lies, not she, but a poor French horse-rider in a travelling circus, so void of friends in those last hours on her hospital bed, that there was none to ask after her, nor tell her name. If all were to be told, perhaps, the tidings would distress the rector most, of all the world. With such a man, " the letter killeth ;" and notwithstanding Jenny's innocence, the thought that for that dreadful year she had been no lawful wife, would have shocked him to the core. There was a time, when, sore at heart, he had thought of joining a certain Anglo-Catholic Retreat, wherein the office of warden had been offered him ; but there was too much good stuff—real substance—in him for that. He remained at Swansdale, to baptise Jenny's first child, and to stand godfather to her second, the girl. And next to Jack Adair —kind, wholesome Jack, to whom Heaven has denied children of his own, for his one child died in infancy, in order, perchance, that his large heart should know no bounds

—the most rapturously received visitor to the nursery, the guest most welcome to the father, most honoured by the mother, at Swansdale Hall, is Mr. Glyddon.

THE END.

BILLING, PRINTER, GUILDFORD, SURREY

www.ingramcontent.com/pod-product-compliance
Lightning Source LLC
Chambersburg PA
CBHW020512270326
41926CB00008B/843